Cambridge English: Proficiency 1

C000252586

WITHOUT ANSWERS

Authentic examination papers from Cambridge ESOL

CAMBRIDGE
UNIVERSITY PRESS

CAMBRIDGE
UNIVERSITY PRESS

University Printing House, Cambridge CB2 8BS, United Kingdom

One Liberty Plaza, 20th Floor, New York, NY 10006, USA

477 Williamstown Road, Port Melbourne, VIC 3207, Australia

314–321, 3rd Floor, Plot 3, Splendor Forum, Jasola District Centre, New Delhi – 110025, India

79 Anson Road, #06–04/06, Singapore 079906

Cambridge University Press is part of the University of Cambridge.

It furthers the University's mission by disseminating knowledge in the pursuit of education, learning and research at the highest international levels of excellence.

www.cambridge.org
Information on this title: www.cambridge.org/9781107609532

© Cambridge University Press 2012

It is normally necessary for written permission for copying to be obtained in advance from a publisher. The candidate answer sheets at the back of this book are designed to be copied and distributed in class. The normal requirements are waived here and it is not necessary to write to Cambridge University Press for permission for an individual teacher to make copies for use within his or her own classroom. Only those pages which carry thewording '© UCLES 2012 Photocopiable' may be copied.

First published 2012
Reprinted 2018

Printed in Italy by Rotolito S.p.A.

A catalogue record for this publication is available from the British Library

ISBN 978-1-107-609532 Student's Book without answers
ISBN 978-1-107-695047 Student's Book with answers
ISBN 978-1-107-637467 Audio CD Set
ISBN 978-1-107-691643 Self-study Pack

Cambridge University Press has no responsibility for the persistence or accuracy of URLs for external or third-party internet websites referred to in this publication, and does not guarantee that any content on such websites is, or will remain, accurate or appropriate. Information regarding prices, travel timetables, and other factual information given in this work is correct at the time of first printing but Cambridge University Press does not guarantee the accuracy of such information thereafter.

Contents

Thanks and acknowledgements

The authors and publishers acknowledge the following sources of copyright material and are grateful for the permissions granted. While every effort has been made, it has not always been possible to identify the sources of all the material used, or to trace all copyright holders. If any omissions are brought to our notice, we will be happy to include the appropriate acknowledgements on reprinting.

Prospect Magazine for the text on p. 14 adapted from 'Oh tell me the truth about beauty' by Jonathan Rée, *Prospect* 1/3/09. Reproduced with permission; Tribune Media Services for the text on pp. 16–17 adapted from 'A Sunshade for the Planet' by David L Chandler, *New Scientist* 21/7/07. Copyright © 2007 Reed Business Information – UK. All rights reserved. Distributed by Tribune Media Services; Guardian News & Media Ltd for the text on p. 19 adapted from 'The Debutants' by Elizabeth Day, *The Observer* 16/1/11, for the text on p. 34 adapted from 'Inside IT' by Bobbie Johnson *The Guardian* 19/12/09, for the text on pp. 36–37 adapted from 'Frame at last' by Leo Benedictus, *The Guardian* 4/11/06, for the text on p. 50 adapted from 'Neologisms' by Henry Hitchings, *The Guardian* 5/2/11, for the text on p. 74 'Less is more' by Stuart Jeffries, *The Guardian* 11/2/11. Copyright © Guardian News & Media Ltd, 2011, 2009, 2006; The Management Lab for text on p. 39 adapted from 'Work-life balance' HYPERLINK "http://www.managementlab.org" www.managementlab.org. Reproduced with permission; Project for Public Spaces for the text on p. 54 adapted from 'Libraries that Matter' by Cynthia Nikitin and Josh Jackson. Copyright © PPS. Reproduced with permission; Telegraph Media Group for the text on pp. 56–57 adapted from 'A wet and wonderful ride in the wild' by Cameron Wilson, *The Telegraph* 4/1/04, for the text on pp. 76–77 adapted from 'Psychology: Just common sense?' by Aisling Irwin, *The Telegraph* 21/10/98. Copyright © Telegraph Media Group Limited, 2004, 1998; NI Syndication for the text on p. 59 adapted from 'Called to the barre' by Abigail Hoffman, *The Times* 24/1/04, for the text on p. 79 adapted from 'What is poetry?' by A A Gill, *Sunday Times* 8/3/09. Copyright © Times Newspapers Limited, 2004, 2009.

The publishers are grateful to the following for permission to include photographs:

Black & White Section:

p. 11 and 71: Thinkstock

Colour Section:

p. C2 (T): © DC Premiumstock/Alamy; p. C2 (B), C4 (TR), C5 (B) and C6 (B): Thinkstock; p. C3 (T): © NHPA/SuperStock; p. C3 (B): Image Source; p. C4 (TL): © Peter Phipp/Travelshots.com/Alamy; p. C4 (C): Getty Images/Ricky John Molloy; p. C4 (B): © Stuart Walker/Alamy; p. C5 (T): Getty Images/Zero Creatives; p. C6 (T): Sipa Press/Rex Features; p. C6 (C): iStockphoto/© Izabela Habur; p. C7 (T): Copyright Guardian News & Media Ltd 2011; p. C7 (B): © age fotostock/SuperStock; p. C8 (T): © Paul Rodriguez/ZUMA Press/Corbis; p. C8 (C): © Cn Boon/Alamy; p. C8 (B): © Frances Roberts/Alamy; p. C9 (T): iStockphoto/© Marcelo Piotti; p. C9 (B): Shutterstock/Specta.

The recordings which accompany this book were made at dsound, London.

Introduction

This collection of four complete practice tests comprises papers from the Cambridge English: Proficiency (CPE) examination; students can practise with these tests on their own or with the help of a teacher.

The CPE examination is part of a suite of general English examinations produced by Cambridge ESOL. This suite consists of five examinations that have similar characteristics but are designed for different levels of English language ability. Within the five levels, CPE is at Level C2 in the Council of Europe's *Common European Framework of Reference for Languages: Learning, teaching, assessment.* It has been accredited by Ofqual, the statutory regulatory authority in England, at Level 3 in the National Qualifications Framework. CPE is recognised by universities, employers, governments and other organisations around the world as proof of the ability to use English to function at the highest levels of academic and professional life.

Examination	Council of Europe Framework Level	UK National Qualifications Framework Level
Cambridge English: Proficiency *Certificate of Proficiency in English (CPE)*	C2	3
Cambridge English: Advanced *Certificate in Advanced English (CAE)*	C1	2
Cambridge English: First *First Certificate in English (FCE)*	B2	1
Cambridge English: Preliminary *Preliminary English Test (PET)*	B1	Entry 3
Cambridge English: Key *Key English Test (KET)*	A2	Entry 2

Further information

The information contained in this practice book is designed to be an overview of the exam. For a full description of all of the above exams including information about task types, testing focus and preparation, please see the relevant handbooks which can be obtained from Cambridge ESOL at the address below or from the website at: www.CambridgeESOL.org

University of Cambridge ESOL Examinations
1 Hills Road
Cambridge CB1 2EU
United Kingdom

Telephone: +44 1223 553355
Fax: +44 1223 460278
e-mail: ESOLHelpdesk@CambridgeESOL.org

The structure of CPE: an overview

The CPE examination consists of four papers:

Reading and Use of English 1 hour 30 minutes
This paper consists of seven parts with 53 questions. For Parts 1 to 4, the test contains texts with accompanying grammar and vocabulary tasks, and discrete items with a grammar and vocabulary focus. For Parts 5 to 7, the test contains texts and accompanying reading comprehension tasks.

Writing 1 hour 30 minutes
This paper consists of two parts which carry equal marks. In Part 1, which is compulsory, candidates must write an essay with a discursive focus of between 240 and 280 words. The task requires candidates to summarise and evaluate the key ideas contained in two texts of approximately 100 words each.

In Part 2, there are five questions from which candidates must choose one to write about. The range of tasks from which questions may be drawn includes an article, a letter, a report, a review, and an essay (set text questions only). The last question (Question 5) is based on the set texts. These set texts remain on the list for two years. Look on the website, or contact the Cambridge ESOL Centre Exams Manager in your area for the up-to-date list of set texts. Question 5 has two options from which candidates choose one to write about. In this part, candidates write between 280 and 320 words.

Assessment is based on the Assessment Scales, comprising four subscales: Content, Communicative Achievement, Organisation, and Language.

Listening 40 minutes (approximately)
This paper consists of four parts with 30 questions. Each part contains a recorded text or texts and corresponding comprehension tasks. Each part is heard twice.

Speaking 16 minutes
The Speaking test consists of three parts. The standard test format is two candidates and two examiners. One examiner acts as interlocutor and manages the interaction either by asking questions or providing cues for the candidates. The other acts as assessor and does not join in the conversation. The test consists of short exchanges with the interlocutor, a collaborative task involving both candidates and an individual long turn followed by a three-way discussion.

Grading
The overall CPE grade is based on the total score gained in all four papers. All candidates receive a Statement of Results which includes a graphical profile of their performance in all four skills and Use of English. Certificates are given to

candidates who pass the examination with grade A, B or C. Candidates whose performance is below C2 level, but falls within Level C1, receive a Cambridge English certificate stating they have demonstrated ability at C1 level. Candidates whose performance falls below Level C1 do not receive a certificate.

For further information on grading and results, go to the website (see page 5).

Test 1

READING AND USE OF ENGLISH (1 hour 30 minutes)

Part 1

For questions **1–8**, read the text below and decide which answer (**A**, **B**, **C** or **D**) best fits each gap.

Mark your answers **on the separate answer sheet**.

There is an example at the beginning (**0**).

0 **A** radically	**B** centrally	**C** sweepingly	**D** rationally

0	A	B	C	D
	▃	▁	▁	▁

The changing role of librarians

A combination of new technology and shifting student expectations is **(0)** ...A.... altering the job of a college or university librarian. Many librarians now regard themselves as information brokers who **(1)** .... and manage access to the information resources needed for learning, teaching and research. They agree that the pace of change has **(2)** .... and much more content is delivered electronically.

As a result of this, a librarian's responsibilities include information technology, knowledge management and institutional portals, in addition to being excellent managers and interpreters of services which may be provided from a growing **(3)** .... of global resources. Despite tremendous changes within library environments, these **(4)** .... are regarded as stimulating. Librarians respond by being flexible and adaptable in establishing a strong customer **(5)** ...., requiring the expansion of their skills to providing **(6)** .... to internet users and delivering e-services. **(7)** ...., most librarians say that many traditional library skills are still **(8)** .... in the digital world.

1 **A** enable   **B** facilitate   **C** incorporate   **D** render

2 **A** accelerated   **B** gathered   **C** raced   **D** hastened

3 **A** accumulation   **B** extent   **C** series   **D** range

4 **A** goals   **B** challenges   **C** achievements   **D** strengths

5 **A** point   **B** attention   **C** focus   **D** contact

6 **A** encouragement   **B** approval   **C** support   **D** supplies

7 **A** Moreover   **B** Nevertheless   **C** Similarly   **D** Therefore

8 **A** applicable   **B** expedient   **C** preferable   **D** parallel

Part 2

For questions **9–16**, read the text below and think of the word which best fits each space. Use only **one** word in each space. There is an example at the beginning (**0**). Write your answers **IN CAPITAL LETTERS on the separate answer sheet.**

Example: | **0** | N | O | T | H | I | N | G | | | | | | | | | |

Why climb mountains?

There's (**0**) .NOTHING. more likely to irritate a mountaineer or explorer than to ask them why they do it, or why they are so willing to put (**9**) .... with danger and discomfort. In 1924 when George Mallory was asked why he wanted to climb Mount Everest, he replied: 'Because it's there.' It may be that, having been asked the same question several hundred times, Mallory just didn't care any more and this was the first phrase to (**10**) .... into his head. Then again, for (**11**) .... we know, it was simply his way of saying, 'Why not?'

This might seem self-evident (**12**) .... someone like Mallory. You climb Everest because you can. One way to look at people like mountaineers or explorers, or successful ones at any rate, is to see them (**13**) .... people who have realised what they are good at. When you read their books, more often than (**14**) .... they will come across as people who are (**15**) .... ease with their environment, (**16**) .... alien it might seem to an outsider.

Part 3

For questions **17–24**, read the text below. Use the word given in capitals at the end of some of the lines to form a word that fits in the space in the same line. There is an example at the beginning (**0**). Write your answers **IN CAPITAL LETTERS on the separate answer sheet**.

Example: | 0 | P | A | R | A | S | I | T | I | C | | | | | | | |

RAFFLESIA

Rafflesia is a rare **(0)** ...PARASITIC... plant species found in Southeast Asia. *Rafflesia* has been **(17)** .... to a fungus because it lacks chlorophyll and is incapable of photosynthesis. Perhaps the only part of *Rafflesia* that is discernible as distinctly plant-like is the flower, which is said to be the world's largest.

PARASITE

LIKE

Many **(18)** .... have been keen to discover why the flower is so large, so they recently conducted **(19)** .... analysis on the plant. This resulted in the **(20)** .... that it has evolved almost 80 times from its origin as a tiny bud to today's seven-kilo mega-bloom. Although this **(21)** .... transformation took tens of millions of years, such an evolutionary spurt is still one of the most dramatic size changes ever reported. Such growth rates in humans would be **(22)** .... to us being 146 metres tall today.

BOTANY

MOLECULE

REVEAL

ORDINARY

COMPARE

The plant is also unusual in another way. Its smell is extremely **(23)** .... but this horrible trait attracts such pollinators as flies. It is thought that *Rafflesia's* huge flower helps radiate the smell over long **(24)** ....

PLEASE

DISTANT

11

Part 4

For questions **25–30**, complete the second sentence so that it has a similar meaning to the first sentence, using the word given. **Do not change the word given.** You must use between **three** and **eight** words, including the word given. Here is an example (**0**).

Example:

0 Do you mind if I watch you while you paint?

objection

Do you .... you while you paint?

0	have any objection to my watching

Write **only** the missing words **on the separate answer sheet**.

---

25 The thing I'd like most would be to visit the art gallery again.

more

There's .... the art gallery again.

26 When I shouted at the boys to stop throwing stones they completely ignored me.

took

The boys .... when I shouted at them to

stop throwing stones.

27 What the lecturer said was not very clear at times.

lack

There .... in what the lecturer said

at times.

28 It was only when it got dark that Paolo decided to make his way back home.

fell

It was not .... that Paolo decided to make his way back

home.

29 The company avoids employing unqualified staff unless there is no alternative.

resort

Only .... employ unqualified staff.

30 The careful preparation for the event ensured it was a memorable day for everyone who

attended.

which

The care .... event ensured it was a

memorable day for everyone.

Part 5

You are going to read a review of a recent book. For questions **31–36**, choose the answer (**A**, **B**, **C** or **D**) which you think fits best according to the text. Mark your answers **on the separate answer sheet**.

Joanna Knight reviews Roger Scruton's book 'Beauty'

Roger Scruton's new book 'Beauty' is a lucid and often graceful compendium of his reflections. He discusses beauty in nature and art, and above all in buildings. Even in an artistic paradise like the city of Venice, Scruton's attention moves quickly from the heroic buildings on the waterfronts to the 'modest neighbours' that surround them. 'Ravishing beauties,' he says, 'are less important in the aesthetics of architecture than those that create a soothing context, a continuous narrative as in a street or a square, where nothing stands out in particular.'

Beauty may have its roots in sensuous enjoyment, but even at its humblest it appeals to something larger: a willingness to consider, compare and arrive at a judgement. The 'judgement of taste', as the philosopher Immanuel Kant called it, spans two worlds: a private world of individual subjectivity, as idiosyncratic as you please, and a public world where you defend and develop your tastes through conscientious discussion – where you try to reason me out of wearing a yellow shirt, for instance, and I try to persuade you to get rid of the Carmen ringtone on your phone.

Scruton explores beauty in its various forms, starting with nature. He maintains, for instance, that the beauty of unspoilt wilderness depends on an evident absence of any fixed centre, a lack of prescribed edges. The beauty of birds, animals and flowers, on the other hand, is rooted in their existence as self-defining entities with boundaries of their own. And the special beauty of the human body belongs not to a mere assemblage of body parts but to the personality that finds expression in it. All this beauty gives you, as Scruton puts it, a sense that 'a world that makes room for such things makes room for you.'

Gardens are different again. They are places where wild nature has been disciplined, more or less sympathetically, into artificial forms. Their beauty is not that of infinite landscapes but of bounded spaces that surround us, rather like architectural interiors; and they enable Scruton to move smoothly from considering natural beauty to the far more contentious terrain of high art. Scruton can be as perceptive about sculpture, painting and classical music as about the varieties of natural beauty, but inevitably he is more controversial.

It is curious to observe how Scruton's feelings lead him to transgress his own standards of courtesy and decorum, and indeed of accurate and well-tuned prose. And you do not have to be a complete punk to suspect that the cause of his anguish may lie within him, and particularly in his premise that there is an unbroken continuum between the beauties of nature and works of art. Any attempt to cover the entire spectrum of reasonable pleasure with a single concept of beauty is bound, after all, to be quite a stretch.

Take the literary arts. Scruton is conspicuously vague when he invokes the concept of 'beautiful novels', and he sounds distinctly uneasy when describing story and dialogue as 'sensory features' of fiction, as if they could appeal to the same aesthetic sense as glorious sunsets. Yet, in the case of literature, beauty is only half the story, and this applies to other art forms too. In a revealing passage, Scruton confesses to a general dislike for cinema as an art form, but he makes one exception: you could take a still from any film by Ingmar Bergman, he says, frame it and hang it on your wall, and it would hold its own there like a picture. That may or may not be true; but single, silent images, however beautiful, are hardly a promising basis for understanding cinematic techniques or judging how they may have extended the ancient arts of storytelling.

Scruton sometimes reminds me of R G Collingwood, one of the most gifted philosophers of the 20th century, with a marvellous sense of history and, apart from a weakness for irritable sarcasm, a wonderful way with words. Like Scruton, he worked out his philosophical ideas in constant engagement with the arts. Unlike him, though, he was aware that there is more to art than beauty. In his autobiography, he described how he came to realise that works of art, however beautiful, will fail if they are unreal or imperceptive; and that works that disappoint lovers of beauty may still articulate issues about the world. If a work does not achieve beauty, it may still bear witness to truth.

31 In describing the buildings of Venice, Scruton reveals his belief that

    A they are less beautiful than some architects claim.

    B some of the streets lack anything of aesthetic value.

    C a harmonious whole is crucial in architecture.

    D beauty can be oppressive if it is overdone.

32 What point is being made in the third paragraph?

    A None of us should feel excluded from notions of beauty.

    B Physical beauty is no indication of character.

    C Observing wild creatures gives us a true sense of what beauty is.

    D Landscape is only beautiful if nothing man-made is visible.

33 The reviewer thinks Scruton's discussion of gardens

    A provides an opportunity for him to condemn artificiality.

    B allows him to emphasise the importance of discipline.

    C acts as a link between two different aspects of the broader topic.

    D balances the previous section on wild nature.

34 How can the reviewer's argument in the sixth paragraph best be summarised?

    A Including a section on works of art was a mistake.

    B The assumption about beauty underlying the book is flawed.

    C Scruton had difficulty fitting all his conflicting ideas on beauty into the book.

    D Scruton's normal writing style is inappropriate for a book of this type.

35 What is the reviewer's opinion of Scruton's section on the cinema?

    A The idea of displaying a still from a film is imaginative.

    B His coverage of film as an art form is inadequate.

    C He is right to concentrate on the beauty of Bergman's films.

    D Describing film as an extension of story-telling is exaggerated.

36 In the final paragraph, why does the reviewer refer to R G Collingwood?

    A to suggest that Scruton was not sufficiently involved in the arts

    B to point out the importance of taking history into account

    C to indicate how Scruton should have widened his view of art

    D to compare the two writers' fondness for sarcasm

Part 6

You are going to read a magazine article about techno-solutions to global warming. Seven paragraphs have been removed from the extract. Choose from the paragraphs **A–H** the one which fits each gap (**37–43**). There is one extra paragraph which you do not need to use. Mark your answers **on the separate answer sheet**.

Cooling the Earth

As a last resort to combat global warming, researchers are investigating two possible ways of applying 'sunscreen' to the planet.

Even with the best will in the world, reducing our carbon emissions is not going to prevent global warming. It has become clear that even if we take the most drastic measures to curb emissions, the uncertainties in our climate models still leave open the possibility of extreme warming and rises in sea level. At the same time, resistance by governments and special interest groups makes it quite possible that the actions advocated by climate scientists might not be implemented soon enough. Is the game up in that case?

37

Quite recently a growing number of researchers have been taking a fresh look at large-scale 'geo-engineering' projects that might be used to counteract global warming. Basically the idea is to apply 'sunscreen' to the whole planet. It's controversial, but recent studies suggest there are ways to deflect just enough of the sunlight reaching the Earth's surface to counteract global warming. Climate models show that blocking just 1.8 per cent of the incident energy in the sun's rays would cancel out the warming effects produced by a doubling of carbon dioxide and other gases in the atmosphere. That could be crucial, because even the most stringent emissions-control measures being suggested would leave us with a doubling of carbon dioxide by the end of this century, and that would last for at least a century more.

38

There are two distinct proposals: reflecting away sunlight within the Earth's atmosphere, or blocking it in outer space. Each approach has its supporters and detractors. While tinkering with the atmosphere is likely to be much cheaper and simpler, space-based approaches may be longer-lasting and less likely to cause unwanted side effects – though they are much more technically challenging.

39

In addition, since it is naturally present at great heights above the earth, some researchers think an increase might not present as many unforeseen risks as some other suggested remedies for global warming, such as seeding the ocean with iron filings or other nutrients to encourage the growth of carbon-consuming organisms.

40

These drawbacks have driven others to look seriously at larger-scale, more expensive alternatives that might carry fewer risks. One that might do the trick is a space-based sunshade system. It may sound wildly implausible but some scientists are convinced that it is feasible.

41

These simple devices would be packed into metal containers in stacks of a million and propelled into space using electromagnetic rail guns – a method that has been tested in labs but never actually used. The acceleration is far too rapid for people or delicate equipment, but the method has long been proposed for shooting bulk material into space, such as water, rocket fuel or building materials. It could be cheaper and more reliable than traditional rockets.

42

Independent computer simulations show that the space sunshade could almost cancel out the temperature changes expected from global warming, except for a small area around each pole. That's because while greenhouse warming is uniform, the poles receive less sunlight than the tropics, so the effect of changes in sunlight is weakest at the poles. This regional difference in cooling might cause unpredictable changes in weather patterns. And since the poles would see less of an effect from the dimming, they might still experience a significant loss of ice cover.

43

Nobody wants to have to do this but if you get to the point where the alternative is six metres of sea-level

rise, we might want to have this as an option. We're not going to implement it, but you certainly have to know what's possible. It's like emergency back-up surgery: you never want to do it, but you still have to practise it.

A The idea is to manufacture discs of silicon about 60 centimetres across. Each disc would be studded with holes of precisely calculated sizes, close to the wavelengths of visible light, which would scatter incoming light like a lens. The effect would be to produce a slight but imperceptible dimming of sunlight.

B So, is the concept of a technological fix new? Not at all; but while most remedies have focused on combating greenhouse gases themselves – finding ways to remove them from the air or scrub them from power-plant emissions – only recently have more radical ideas been taken seriously.

C Well, fortunately, if the worst comes to the worst, scientists still have a few tricks up their sleeves. For the most part they have strongly resisted discussing these options for fear of inviting a sense of complacency that might thwart efforts to tackle the root of the problem. Until now, that is.

D What's more, geo-engineering in general has major drawbacks. It does nothing about the carbon dioxide in the atmosphere, which would still produce effects such as ocean acidification. When carbonic acid runs into the oceans from rocks, they get more acidic. Nobody disputes that this will happen on an increasing scale. The only question is how much it matters to basic ecosystems.

E The simplest method put forward has been known for decades. That is to inject sulphur dioxide into the stratosphere, mimicking the cooling effects of volcanoes. Sulphur is cheap, and the means of releasing it could be as simple as pumping it up through a vertical pipe as much as ten kilometres long. Sulphur dioxide forms sulphate particles that are big enough to block part of the incoming sunlight, but small enough to allow infrared wavelengths – the heat radiation from the Earth – to escape back into space.

F So, which approach has the edge? It comes down to costs and feasibility. If we were suddenly faced with a climate catastrophe, the sulphur-particle approach is cheap enough to be essentially free. The engineering is simple enough that it could be put up in a couple of years. The space sunshade, though attractive, seems unlikely to be implemented. If cost were no object, one would want to use something like this latter scheme, because it's very clean and controllable, and would likely minimise any secondary effects. But it's very expensive. If you want to go to that much effort, it would be simpler just to change our energy systems.

G The approach is not without side-effects, however. Anything we do within the Earth's atmosphere might have unpredictable results that turn out to be worse than the cure, such as dramatic changes in regional rainfall or drought patterns, or chemical reactions that might disrupt ecosystems.

H Once launched, the receptacles would travel to the place between the Earth and sun where their gravitational fields cancel out, allowing objects to remain stationary relative to the two bodies. This is where the contents would be released. Scientists think they could be kept in place for 50 years or more.

Part 7

You are going to read a magazine article about six young people who have been successful in various artistic fields. For questions **44–53**, choose from the people (**A–F**). The people may be chosen more than once. Mark your answers **on the separate answer sheet.**

Which of the successful young people

is inspired to investigate motivation? | 44 |

is undaunted by the prospect of future demands? | 45 |

makes a link between background and character? | 46 |

appears to have thrived on negative feedback? | 47 |

seems strangely unassuming given levels of success? | 48 |

concentrates more on the medium than the message? | 49 |

was prepared to make a leap into the unknown? | 50 |

owes success to taking a step on impulse? | 51 |

has a healthy disregard for adverse comment? | 52 |

shows an understanding way beyond experience? | 53 |

Six to watch

Sarah Carter chooses six young people to watch in various artistic fields.

A Yasmin Shahmir – singer

'I was so excited. I felt euphoric,' says Yasmin having heard her first single being played. After five years spent DJing, this is one milestone the 22 year-old will never forget. The feline-eyed singer cuts a striking figure and you sense she was not destined to stay behind the decks forever. 'The song is about a time in my life when I was really going out on a limb – I'd quit my university course and moved to London where I was up for whatever life threw at me. At school I'd never been like the others – I'm half-Iranian, half-English and have a weird name. So I stood out a bit – maybe that's where my determined attitude comes from.'

B Emma Hart – video artist

Emma Hart is tipped as 'one-to-watch'. Her output consists of video works, lectures and performances that challenge the way photographs and film are received. They make witty observations about everyday situations and ask the viewer to be active and questioning. 'The focus,' she says, 'is on how I use the camera, not on what I'm filming.' Recognition has been hard won. She worked first as a 'frustrated' office clerk. Bitten by the photography bug, she began a degree course but, constantly getting marked down on technical issues, dropped out. However, the criticism received was probably the making of her – it helped consolidate her artistic ideas, and made her more determined. It paid off in the end.

C Danielle Hope – actor

'I'm 18, I'm a leading lady and a singer. I mean, who'd have thought it?' Danielle's life has undergone a considerable change – last year she was working as a waitress and thinking about applying to drama school. Instead, she auditioned on a whim and beat 9,000 hopefuls to win the lead role in a forthcoming musical. She seems remarkably unfazed by the task ahead. 'I don't want to let anyone down. It's self-pressure more than anything. Of course some will like my performance, some will hate it. Everyone's entitled to their opinion. I won't take it to heart – they won't be criticising me the person, but me the actress. It's all been so exciting – I've no idea what's going to be next.'

D Eudon Choi – fashion designer

Eudon Choi trained as a menswear designer in South Korea and has always enjoyed the support of his family. After moving to London he won a prestigious award and his collection is soon to be stocked in 'Brown's Focus', an influential fashion boutique. For all the accolades, Eudon is surprisingly diffident. Is it a strain living up to all the hype? 'You can say that again.' For a relatively new designer, it's a great start. His inspiration comes from eclectic sources – he trawls vintage shops for military jackets and has, in the past, taken the aesthetic of the industrial revolution as his model. Now his clothes are acclaimed by fashion editors and worn by celebrities.

E Andrew Sheridan – playwright

Andrew Sheridan's debut play is soon to open in Manchester. It has already been described as 'the best first play' by one of a group of leading young playwrights, the friends who initially pushed him into writing. It will be judged by the actors too, well known to Sheridan after a decade performing on stage and screen, and by his family. His family's reaction concerns him – none of them has ever had anything to do with the theatre and they haven't read his play. A desire to delve into 'what it is to be human' primarily drives his writing – 'what ultimately makes us tick.' Will his family find it all a bit weird?

F Sunjeev Sahota – novelist

Sunjeev studied maths at university and didn't catch the reading bug until relatively late – he didn't read a novel until he was 18. Now, after eleven years spent 'catching-up', with his own first novel just published, he talks with the air of someone with a lifetime's reading behind him. It took him four years to write, working in the evenings and at weekends, but he didn't really expect to get it published – 'It was just maybe, maybe.' Now that it's out, he feels good. 'My friends aren't readers. They're just normal lads. But they've all bought the book. I'm anxious, slightly, and proud.'

WRITING (1 hour 30 minutes)

Part 1

Read the two texts below.

Write an essay summarising and evaluating the key points from both texts. Use your own words throughout as far as possible, and include your own ideas in your answers.

Write your answer in **240–280** words.

1

The Effects of Music

We humans are a musical species no less than a linguistic one. This takes many different forms. All of us (with very few exceptions) can perceive music, harmony and rhythm. We integrate all of these using many different parts of the brain. And to this largely unconscious appreciation of music is added an often intense and profound emotional reaction. Shakespeare referred to music as the 'food of love', and for most people their lives would be the poorer without music. Music is capable of stimulating both passion and compassion, speaking to our very core and taking us to the heights and depths of emotion.

Music in Schools?

There is little doubt that regular exposure to music, and especially active participation in music, may stimulate development of other abilities. Some argue that music is as important educationally as reading or writing, and suggest that a musical education advantages those with mathematical aptitude. What people do not agree about, however, is which kind of music is the most educationally valuable. Some regard classical music as the only kind of music that should be taught in schools. However, leaving aside the problem of defining 'classical' in different cultural contexts, there is a strong case that all types of music are equally valid in stimulating an individual's potential.

Write your **essay**.

Part 2

Write an answer to **one** of the questions **2–5** in this part. Write your answer in **280–320** words in an appropriate style.

---

2 You have read an article in an international magazine on the topic of friendship. The magazine has asked readers to respond with their views. You decide to write a letter. In your letter you should briefly describe a special friendship that is important to you and assess the difficulties of maintaining friendships over time and in changing circumstances.

Write your **letter**.

3 An English-language magazine has invited readers to send in reviews about a TV programme which has deepened their understanding of a particular country and its culture. You decide to send in a review of such a TV programme. You should briefly describe the programme and explain how it affected your views on the country and its culture.

Write your **review**.

4 You work for the tourist office in your area. Your manager has asked you to write a report in English on a park that is popular with tourists. You should briefly describe the facilities that are currently available to visitors. Your report should also recommend two or three improvements that would enhance the park further and explain why these would attract even more visitors.

Write your **report**.

5 Write an answer to **one** of the following two questions based on **one** of the titles below. Write **5(a)** or **5(b)** at the beginning of your answer.

(a) Marc Norman and Tom Stoppard: *Shakespeare in Love*
An international magazine is planning a series of articles on love and marriage at different times in history. You decide to contribute an article on *Shakespeare in Love*. You should briefly describe Viola's relationships with Will and Wessex and explain how money and position in society influence the three characters' attitudes to love.

Write your **article**.

(b) Philip K Dick: *Do Androids Dream of Electric Sheep?*
'I want to have an animal; I keep trying to buy one. But on my salary…' Your tutor asks you to write an essay on the status of animals in *Do Androids Dream of Electric Sheep?*, evaluating the importance of real and electric animals to the society in which Rick lives. You should refer to events in the story to support your views.

Write your **essay**.

LISTENING (40 minutes approximately)

Part 1

You will hear three different extracts.

For questions **1–6**, choose the answer (**A**, **B** or **C**) which fits best according to what you hear. There are two questions for each extract.

> **Extract One**

You hear two careers advisers discussing whether students should take a year off after graduation to go travelling.

1 When mentioning recent statistics on graduates taking gap years, the man reveals

    A   his scepticism about the value of rushing to get a job after university.

    B   his doubts about the validity of some research.

    C   his understanding of the anxiety that prevents them from travelling.

2 What do the two careers advisers agree about a gap year?

    A   Some employers consider it a lazy option.

    B   The way graduates present it at interview is crucial.

    C   Graduates should spend it doing something relevant to their career.

> **Extract Two**

You hear a sociologist talking about consumer buying behaviour.

3 What does the sociologist say about the 'information search stage' of decision making?

    A   It arouses a desire for a better situation.

    B   It is likely to be incomplete.

    C   It is a lengthy process.

4 According to the sociologist, how do marketing professionals most successfully influence people's choice of product?

    A   They aim to create new aspirations in people.

    B   They offer updated designs that increase customer satisfaction.

    C   They improve websites to make buying their products easy.

Extract Three

You hear a man who has an internet company talking about selling goods online.

5 In the man's opinion, what is most needed when selling goods online?

   A   an appreciation of how it differs from shop-based selling
   B   a willingness to adapt quickly to new circumstances
   C   an awareness of how to make a website attractive

6 What is the man doing in answer to the interviewer's question about growing an online business?

   A   comparing the advantages of two business theories
   B   warning of the dangers of inadequate funding
   C   suggesting the use of external consultants

Part 2

You will hear a student, Hannah Jorden, giving a short talk on the topic of soil.

For questions **7–15**, complete the sentences with a word or short phrase.

Hannah has found out that people have used soil as a **(7)** ....
for thousands of years.

Hannah says that the increase in **(8)** .... is putting pressure
on the way we use soil.

Pollutants from waste in the soil can enter the **(9)** ....
and can affect both plants and humans.

Hannah has found evidence showing that waste pollution reduces the number of
(10) .... in the soil.

The main cause of inorganic pollution is the **(11)** .... which takes
place in many countries.

Hannah is interested in the fact that organic pollutants can directly affect the
(12) .... in humans.

Hannah gives the example of **(13)** .... as a natural cause of acid
rain.

Hannah has found that soil erosion caused by **(14)** .... has been
of interest to the media.

Soil has become less fertile owing to the method known as
(15) ....

Part 3

You will hear part of a discussion programme, in which a teacher called Simon and a business journalist called Trina are talking about the issue of change.

For questions **16–20**, choose the answer (**A**, **B**, **C** or **D**) which fits best according to what you hear.

16   What does Simon say about change when discussing linguistic expressions?

A   It is an inevitable part of life.

B   It is generally perceived as unwelcome.

C   Its significance has altered over time.

D   It brings improvements when they're least expected.

17   What do they agree about change in the business community?

A   It is regarded as synonymous with progress.

B   It is seen as unfortunate but necessary.

C   It never seems to be questioned.

D   It can lead to undesirable results.

18   What does Trina dislike about feedback forms?

A   the scale of the reaction they can provoke

B   the disharmony they can create within organisations

C   the extent of their use in the world of education

D   the justification they give to managers who want to introduce changes

19   When discussing day-to-day routines, Simon and Trina agree that people

A   make too much fuss about small-scale changes.

B   find that changes in the workplace mirror those in daily life.

C   only like change that clearly benefits them personally.

D   experience an ongoing cycle of resisting and accepting change.

20   In Simon's view, people will really enjoy an activity if

A   they do it on a regular basis.

B   they keep on changing it slightly.

C   it represents a change for them.

D   it coincides with their expectations.

Part 4

You will hear five short extracts in which people are talking about their involvement in award-winning projects related to the natural world.

TASK ONE

For questions **21–25**, choose from the list (**A–H**) what special feature of the project each speaker mentions.

TASK TWO

For questions **26–30**, choose from the list (**A–H**) what positive effect of receiving the award each speaker appreciated.

While you listen, you must complete both tasks.

A a combination of old and new methods	**A** Advanced technology was donated.
B the involvement of community leaders	**B** The original idea was improved.
C the recycling of local resources	**C** Critics of the project were silenced.
D the adaptation of space technology	**D** The attitude of local people changed.
E an idea copied from another part of the world	**E** Related information could be shared.
F the use of a different material	**F** More staff were taken onto the project.
G a method based on an accidental discovery	**G** Awareness of endangered species was increased.
H the development of a single multi-purpose system	**H** The economy of the region was developed.

TASK ONE		TASK TWO	
Speaker 1	21	Speaker 1	26
Speaker 2	22	Speaker 2	27
Speaker 3	23	Speaker 3	28
Speaker 4	24	Speaker 4	29
Speaker 5	25	Speaker 5	30

SPEAKING (16 minutes)

There are two examiners. One (the interlocutor) conducts the test, providing you with the necessary materials and explaining what you have to do. The other examiner (the assessor) will be introduced to you, but then takes no further part in the interaction.

Part 1 (2 minutes)

The interlocutor first asks you and your partner a few questions which focus on information about yourselves.

Part 2 (4 minutes)

In this part of the test you and your partner are asked to talk together. The interlocutor places a set of pictures on the table in front of you. There may be only one picture in the set or as many as seven pictures. This stimulus provides the basis for a discussion. The interlocutor first asks an introductory question which focuses on two of the pictures (or in the case of a single picture, on aspects of the picture). After about a minute, the interlocutor gives you both a decision-making task based on the same set of pictures.

The pictures for Part 2 are on pages C2–C3 of the colour section.

Part 3 (10 minutes)

You are each given the opportunity to talk for two minutes, to comment after your partner has spoken and to take part in a more general discussion.

The interlocutor gives you a card with a question written on it and asks you to talk about it for two minutes. After you have spoken, the interlocutor asks you both another question related to the topic on the card, addressing your partner first. This procedure is repeated, so that your partner receives a card and speaks for two minutes and a follow-up question is asked.

Finally, the interlocutor asks some further questions, which leads to a discussion on a general theme related to the subjects already covered in Part 3.

The cards for Part 3 are on pages C10–C11 of the colour section.

Test 2

READING AND USE OF ENGLISH (1 hour 30 minutes)

Part 1

For questions **1–8**, read the text below and decide which answer (**A, B, C** or **D**) best fits each gap.

Mark your answers **on the separate answer sheet**.

There is an example at the beginning (**0**).

| **0** | **A** | in particular | **B** | in any case | **C** | in turn | **D** | in the end |

0	A	B	C	D

Scientists and communication

Scientists are often accused of being poor communicators, yet there are many reasons why scientists, **(0)** ....A...., should be and often are good communicators. After all, science calls **(1)** .... enthusiasm and scientists often possess this **(2)** .... quality in large quantities. Enthusiasm can be infectious, but to command the interest of readers, scientists must develop their other **(3)** .... talents: clarity, observation and knowledge.

Those scientists who are logical thinkers can usually write clearly, and the more clearly thoughts are **(4)** .... , the greater their potential value. In the same way, those who observe must take account of subtle differences for the observations they may **(5)** .... as significant. Finally, those who write must have something of **(6)** .... value to say.

A scientist whose work never sees the **(7)** .... of day has achieved nothing of worth until somebody else hears about it. It is essential, therefore, for scientists to lay to **(8)** .... the myth that they cannot communicate, once and for all.

1 **A** on   **B** up   **C** for   **D** in

2 **A** arresting   **B** engaging   **C** catching   **D** fetching

3 **A** native   **B** innate   **C** standard   **D** typical

4 **A** put across   **B** come over   **C** given out   **D** set up

5 **A** document   **B** predict   **C** enter   **D** pronounce

6 **A** basic   **B** radical   **C** intrinsic   **D** central

7 **A** light   **B** start   **C** dawn   **D** birth

8 **A** sleep   **B** rest   **C** bed   **D** ground

Part 2

For questions **9–16**, read the text below and think of the word which best fits each space. Use only **one** word in each space. There is an example at the beginning **(0)**. Write your answers **IN CAPITAL LETTERS on the separate answer sheet.**

Example: | 0 | O | F |

Film music

Any mention **(0)** ...OF... the movie Star Wars instantly triggers the resounding opening bars of the film score, which signals the presence of the enemy. But can you call to **(9)** .... who wrote the music?

(10) .... to the legendary film director Orson Wells, music accounts **(11)** .... half the work in a movie, mostly **(12)** .... the audience even knowing the composer's name. The cruellest **(13)** .... of it for the composer is that, in a good film, that is how it should be. If the art of dressing well is to all intents and purposes to dress in such a way that others do **(14)** .... notice your elegance, the art of a great music score is to fuse so perfectly with what is on the screen that audiences are unconsciously sucked **(15)** .... the mood of the movie. For this reason, even great movie music brings very **(16)** .... recognition to composers.

Part 3

For questions **17–24**, read the text below. Use the word given in capitals at the end of some of the lines to form a word that fits in the space in the same line. There is an example at the beginning (**0**). Write your answers **IN CAPITAL LETTERS on the separate answer sheet**.

Example: | **0** | B | E | A | U | T | I | F | U | L | L | Y | | | | | | |

Extreme weather

Extreme Weather is packed with facts about the great forces of nature
and is a **(0)** ..BEAUTIFULLY.. illustrated science book by   **BEAUTY**
the meteorologist, H. Michael Mogil. The aim of the book is to present
enough knowledge to understand the many **(17)** ……..... of the debate   **COMPLEX**
about climate change.

Mogil is alarmed about the way the public has been **(18)** ……..... on this issue,   **LEAD**
being pushed towards certain positions on climate change by the
campaigning of **(19)** ……..... and the news media's need for a good   **POLITICS**
story. He wants to demonstrate that climate change is an **(20)** ……….   **CREDIBLE**
complicated issue, and that making overly simplistic **(21)** ……….   **ASSUME**
will inevitably **(22)** ……..... our understanding. He therefore   **PAIR**
(23) ……..... emphasises that weather records are short, often   **REPEAT**
incomplete and tricky to compare. Mogil suggests that, in the distant
past, changes in climate occurred in magnitudes far greater than in
recent times. It is the **(24)** ……..... detail with which these recent events   **FINITE**
have been recorded that differentiates them from the past.

Part 4

For questions **25–30**, complete the second sentence so that it has a similar meaning to the first sentence, using the word given. **Do not change the word given.** You must use between **three** and **eight** words, including the word given. Here is an example (**0**).

Example:

0 Do you mind if I watch you while you paint?

objection

Do you .... you while you paint?

0	have any objection to my watching

Write **only** the missing words **on the separate answer sheet**.

---

25 It can be difficult to make a decision when there is too much time to think.

reach

Having too much time to think may .... a decision.

26 Visitors can only enter the exhibition if they have booked online.

restricted

Entrance .... have booked online.

27 If Stevie hadn't acted promptly to put out the fire, there might have been more damage to the kitchen.

in

But .... out the fire, there might have been more damage to the kitchen.

28 Taxes will most probably rise next year.

every

There .... next year.

29 Although she didn't agree with the management's decision, Chloe was forced to accept it.

choice

Much as she disagreed with it, Chloe .... the management's decision.

30 We have taken to going to the cinema on Fridays.

habit

We .... going to the cinema on Fridays.

Part 5

You are going to read a newspaper article about young people and technology. For questions **31–36**, choose the answer (**A**, **B**, **C** or **D**) which you think fits best according to the text. Mark your answers **on the separate answer sheet**.

Young People and Technology

Danah Boyd is a specialist researcher looking at how young people use technology

If there's one cliche that really grates with Danah Boyd, who has made a career from studying the way younger people use the web, it's that of the digital native. 'There's nothing native about young people's engagement with technology,' she says, adamantly. She has little time for the widely held assumption that kids are innately more adept at coping with the web or negotiating the hurdles of digital life. 'Young people are learning about the social world around them,' she says. 'Today that world has computer-mediated communications. Thus, in order to learn about their social world, they're learning about those things too. And they're leveraging that to work out the stuff that kids have always worked out: peer sociality, status, etc.'

It's no surprise she takes exception, really: as one of the first digital anthropologists to dig into the way people use social networking sites, Boyd has a track record of exposing the truths that underpin many of our assumptions about the online world. Along the way, she's gained insights into the social web – not just by conducting studies of how many kids were using social-networking sites, but by taking a closer look at what was going on.

Lately, her work has been about explaining new ways of interpreting the behaviour we see online, and understanding that the context of online activity is often more subtle than we first imagine. She outlined some examples at a recent conference in San Francisco, including the case of a young man from one of the poorest districts of Los Angeles who was applying to a prestigious American college. The applicant said he wanted to escape the influence of gangs and violence, but the admissions officer was appalled when he discovered that the boy's MySpace page was plastered with precisely the violent language and gang imagery he claimed to abhor. Why was he lying about his motivations, asked the university? 'He wasn't,' says Boyd: in his world, showing the right images online was a key part of surviving daily life.

Understanding what's happening online is especially pertinent while discussions rage about how perceptions of privacy are shifting – particularly the idea that today's teenagers have a vastly different approach to privacy from their predecessors. Instead, Boyd says, activities that strike adults as radically new are often more easily understood from the perspective of teenagers. 'Kids have always cared about privacy, it's just that their notions of privacy look very different from adult notions,' she says. 'Kids often don't have the kind of privacy adults assume they do. Adults, by and large, think of the home as a very private space. The thing is, for young people that's often not the case because they have little or no control over who has access to it, or under what conditions. As a result, the online world can feel more private because it feels like there's more control.'

_{line 32} This concept of control is central to Boyd's work, and it applies not only to debunking myths about teenage behaviour, but also to similar ideas that have emerged about the rest of the web. Unlike some prognosticators who preach unstoppable revolution, Boyd suggests that control remains, _{line 34} by and large, in the same places it always did. 'Technologists all go for the notion of "techno-utopia", the web as great democratiser,' she says. 'Sure, we've made creation and distribution more available to anyone, but at the same time we've made those things irrelevant. Now the commodity isn't distribution, it's attention – and guess what? We're not actually democratising the whole system – we're just shifting the way in which we discriminate.'

It's a call to arms that most academic researchers would tend to sidestep, but then Boyd admits to treading a fine line between academic and activist. After all, she adds, part of her purpose is to look at the very questions that make us feel uncomfortable. 'Part of it is that as a researcher, everybody's obsessed with Twitter and Facebook, and we've got amateur research all over the place,' she says. 'Plenty of scholars are jumping in and looking at very specific things. The questions I continue to want to ask are the things that are challenging to me: having to sit down and be forced to think about uncomfortable social stuff, and it's really hard to get my head around it, which means it's exactly what I should dive in and deal with.'

31 What point does Danah Boyd make about 'computer-mediated communications' (line 5)?

    A They set out to teach the young about social interaction.

    B They are an integral part of a young person's social interaction.

    C They act as a barrier to wider social interaction amongst young people.

    D They take the place of other sorts of social interaction for young people.

32 In the second paragraph, what do we learn about Danah's research into social networking sites?

    A It has largely sought to account for their rapid growth.

    B It has tended to question people's attitudes towards them.

    C It has taken the form of in-depth studies into how they are designed.

    D It has begun to investigate whether they are as influential as people think.

33 What point does Danah's example of the Los Angeles college applicant illustrate?

    A how easy it is to misinterpret an individual's online activity

    B how readily somebody's online activity can be investigated

    C what their online activity can tell us about a person's sincerity

    D how important it is to check the content of someone's online activity

34 The phrase 'debunking myths' (line 32) refers to Danah's view that

    A today's teenagers are less concerned about privacy than previous generations.

    B teenagers value the idea of privacy more in a domestic environment.

    C teenagers' attitudes to privacy are changing less than people think.

    D parents tend not to respect teenagers' need for online privacy.

35 Danah uses the term 'techno-utopia' (line 34) to underline her view that

    A her research has resonance for a community of web users of all ages.

    B people have unrealistic expectations about the influence of the web.

    C control of the web remains in much the same hands as before.

    D the web has a largely positive effect on many people's lives.

36 In the last paragraph, we are given the impression that Danah

    A feels that a lot of research about the web is lacking in sufficient detail.

    B is aware that some issues in her field cannot yet be researched fully.

    C regards herself as being more of a philosopher than a researcher.

    D is willing to take on research challenges others would avoid.

Part 6

You are going to read an article about the work of a TV animator. Seven paragraphs have been removed from the extract. Choose from the paragraphs **A–H** the one which fits each gap **(37–43)**. There is one extra paragraph which you do not need to use. Mark your answers **on the separate answer sheet.**

An Animated Life

Adam Farish works in stop-motion animation – the technique of making TV cartoons by manipulating static models rather than using drawings or computers. It might sound a bit childish, but it isn't all child's play. 'I tell people what I do, and they go, "You can't do that. Get a proper job!"' A sheepish grin spreads across the face of Adam Farish, 36, who spends eight hours a day playing with dolls. 'It makes me laugh,' he shrugs. And, on cue, he laughs. It's an explosive, wheezy laugh, a brief eruption of permanently suppressed amusement. Even after three years as an animator, it seems as if he still can't believe his luck.

37	

His company's big project at the moment is the new Rupert Bear series, *Follow the Magic*. Consequently, Farish has spent many months absorbed in Rupert's surreal existence. 'It is acting, but you're not using your own body to act with,' he explains. 'We come in and we have to pretend we're five-year-old toy bears rescuing elephants out of trees. It does something to your head after a while.'

38	

This great mountain of work must all be performed to a minute level of detail, and with complete accuracy. If a character makes a large gesture, for instance, there must always be a slight recoil in the limb before they do it. This must be posed and photographed. Blinking, which a character must do all the time if it is to seem human, involves replacing an open eyelid with a half-closed eyelid and taking a picture, then replacing this with a three-quarter-closed eyelid and taking a picture, then switching to a fully closed one and taking a picture, then putting on the three-quarter one again …

39	

When you factor in all the work done by others in building and lighting the sets correctly and providing each character with their props and costumes, it is easy to see why stop-motion animation has a reputation for being, well, slow. 'We've got a target of 13 seconds a day. Most other companies do three or four, but because we're doing series work and there's tight deadlines, we have to push it to 13 seconds – that is 325 frames in other words. It's quite strange,' he muses, 'because it's so … ,' he searches for the right word, 'dull.'

40	

So, as far as anyone can tell, the knack of getting it right is handed out at birth, and not to many people. Yet despite the rareness of the skill, the animator's job is seldom secure. Most work on short-term contracts (Farish's runs out in May), and, as with so many labour-intensive industries, other countries are taking an ever-increasing share of the business.

41	

Farish grew up in Aldershot, an army town, with a father who believed firmly in discipline. This belief engendered the opposite in his son, who, despite being bright, barely attended school and managed to leave with a bad report and an attitude problem. 'I was a bit mouthy,' he says, 'generally my own fault.'

42	

He survived on what work he could find, moving on from town to town once he'd outstayed his welcome. 'At times, I loved it,' he admits, 'that total freedom from responsibility. And then it starts getting a bit cold, and you think: "Help! How am I going to eat?"'

43	

Now Farish makes £30,000 a year, at least until May, and has never been happier. Despite the insecurity, the boredom, and having to explain what he does all the time, he says he loves his job – especially when the dolls get something exciting to do.

A Because he's known worse, these threats to his livelihood bother Farish less than most. For six years he was homeless, on and off, and even food was not guaranteed. 'I've already hit the lowest you can go,' he says.

B But even this isn't the most laborious process. That honour goes to speech, as every lip and tongue movement for every sound has to be posed and photographed, and the result must synchronise perfectly with the recorded soundtrack. The character may be pointing and simultaneously doing a little dance. Writers, on the whole, are blithely unaware of the nightmare such actions will bring for the poor wretch who translates their imaginations into reality.

C Small, stocky and shaven-headed, Farish does not immediately make one think of children's television. He works in Manchester for Cosgrove Hall, a famous old animation shop responsible for classics such as *Danger Mouse* and *Count Duckula*. The building is a warren of black baize curtains, separating a series of untidy studios. The atmosphere is one of chaos held precariously at bay.

D Towards the end of even the longest day, however, comes the moment that animators live for: pressing 'play'. 'It's a dead object,' says Farish, 'and then all of a sudden it's moving around and talking, and jumping about.' It's as if he is describing some kind of magic spell. 'You can't see until you've done it, so it's all got to be in your head until you're finished, and when you press play – that's when you find out if it all works or not.'

E Having started as a plumber's apprentice in the early 1990s, he found himself without qualifications, and then suddenly without a job when economic recession hit. 'People stopped paying each other, and I was bottom of the chain.' He was left with just a sleeping-bag, a penknife and a change of clothes to depend on.

F In fact, Farish's dedication knows no bounds. He even creates short cartoons in his spare time for his own amusement. Stop-motion is too complex and expensive to do at home, so he is teaching himself computer-generated animation. 'It started off as a bit of light relief but it's gradually taking over home life as well.'

G But then, after a period studying production management at drama school, Farish enrolled on a web-design course. One day they had an animation lesson, and out of 20 students, Farish was the only one who could do it. On his teacher's recommendation, he gave up web design and took a degree in animation. 'I never chose to be an animator,' he says. 'It never occurred to me that you could do this for a job.'

H That would not, of course, be the reaction of a child, but while a child might put a more positive spin on this, no child could muster the prodigious levels of discipline and concentration required to see the job through. All the cartoons are filmed with stop-motion animation so Farish spends his days breaking down the behaviour of his characters into thousands of tiny steps, posing the puppets into each position, and taking a picture of the scene to make a frame of film.

Part 7

You are going to read an article about work-life balance. For questions **44–53**, choose from the sections (**A–D**). The sections may be chosen more than once. Mark your answers **on the separate answer sheet.**

Which section mentions the following?

involvement in decision-making leading to increased worker satisfaction	**44**
a term that was once used to refer to an inadequate work-life balance	**45**
a reduction in one business's expenditure caused by improved staff retention	**46**
a recognition among some employees of the necessity for longer working hours	**47**
changes in the world of work leading to competition between established and emerging companies	**48**
the statutory regulation of work-life balance ideas	**49**
certain staff benefits no longer being seen as adequate by potential employees	**50**
a change in how work-life balance developments are generated	**51**
a way of defining what work-life balance involves	**52**
a theory as to what people require out of life	**53**

Issues arising out of the continuing work-life balance debate in the UK

A

Here in the UK, the continuous pressure of work and the relentless pace of change is impacting on people. Hard. And some people have reached the point where they want their lives back or at least are questioning how they can balance their work obligations with their domestic responsibilities. This includes new recruits – employers also recognise that in the battle to attract talented people the tried and tested incentives of high salary, a medical plan and use of a company car will not pull in the high fliers any more. But what exactly does work-life balance cover? In the recent past, 'stress' was the word that best seemed to represent this general concern about too much work, too little life. Everyone understood it, since they experienced it at a personal level, but work-life balance has larger parameters. According to the Work Foundation, it is only achieved when an individual's right to a fulfilled life inside and outside paid work is respected as the norm. So, for example, work-life balance also takes into account the contribution that people want to make to the world in which they live. It includes the recognition that people have to manage family life and it considers the impact that an excessive workload has on people's health.

B

We can point to the psychologist, Abraham Maslow, as the inspiration behind the work-life balance phenomenon. Maslow's 'hierarchy of needs' model posits five ascending levels of need, each stage of which has to be satisfied in turn before the individual can move onwards and upwards. So, at the base of the triangular model, individuals first have to satisfy their physical survival needs, while at the apex of the triangle, is the 'self-actualised' individual whose priorities are personal growth and fulfilment. Maslow's work fused with a trend that also affected the concerns about work-life balance. Having a job for life, which had been part of the bedrock values of traditional companies, simply could not be sustained by the dynamic marketplace of the 1990s and beyond. The old certainties evaporated, and employers realised that the new imperative was to ensure their employees became as innovative as the young entrepreneurs who were creating exciting new businesses of their own.

C

The idea of a work-life balance has evolved over time. In the UK, there has been a long tradition of government-based initiatives that were its forerunners. However, with work-life balance as it exists today, the influence of some corporate role models has had the most impact. Consider Ben & Jerry's, the US ice-cream company. Since the 1980s, this firm has recognised that people wanted a different sort of work experience. It made a virtue out of donating 7.5 per cent of its pre-tax profits to philanthropy – an employee-led initiative. Engaging employees in such a way has helped both to improve motivation and drive innovation and productivity, making Ben & Jerry's into an extremely lucrative brand. A recent survey identified more than 100 varieties of similar work-life initiatives. However, it is clear that the most important variable in work-life balance is the nature of the job itself. People want jobs with autonomy, flexibility, meaning, managerial support as well as a chance for advancement.

D

So, do work-life balance policies work? In the UK there has been little doubt that they have had a positive impact. British Telecom, for instance, used work-life balance initiatives both to draw more women into the workforce and to address the significant problem of losing staff. As a result, a staggering 98 per cent of women returned after maternity leave, saving the organisation a tidy sum in recruitment and training. Work-life balance is already a catch-all term for many different new policy developments and the list is still growing. Many employees know from direct experience that the world of work is changing. In a 24/7 society, they recognise that their customers expect service round-the-clock. And they also know that they have to juggle their home responsibilities while stretching their schedules to meet customer expectations. Employers know this too. Indeed, there is a raft of legal provisions governing work-life balance being driven by the European Union. And what the individual employee wants and the employer is set to deliver need not be in opposition.

WRITING (1 hour 30 minutes)

Part 1

Read the two texts below.

Write an essay summarising and evaluating the key points from both texts. Use your own words throughout as far as possible, and include your own ideas in your answers.

Write your answer in **240–280** words.

1

> ### Movie magic
>
> It has often been claimed that people flock to the cinema primarily to escape from the boredom, or sometimes even the misery, of their everyday lives. Remarkable technological advances have made the experience of watching a movie ever more magical and emotionally powerful, increasing the appeal and impact of the cinema for each new generation. Yet movies have a power that goes far beyond their capacity to transport us to another world, since they can influence audiences to change their attitudes or behaviour in significant ways, making them consider complex moral and social issues such as war, poverty, and prejudice.

> ### Is the cinema in decline?
>
> The inescapable truth is that the cinema, one of the greatest cultural achievements of the twentieth century, has reached a new low point in recent years. All but a few movies are, frankly, not worth anyone's valuable time. Audiences are increasingly presented with childish comedies, predictable action films and disappointing sequels. There is also the absurd idea that a film with an inflated budget of millions is a substitute for a well-acted, imaginative and original film. Film studios now spend almost as much money on marketing their films as producing them, which tends to suggest their concern is with profit rather than quality.

Write your **essay**.

Part 2

Write an answer to **one** of the questions **2–5** in this part. Write your answer in **280–320** words in an appropriate style.

---

2   You are a student at an international college. Your tutor has asked you to write an article for the college website on ways students can improve language skills outside the classroom. In your article, you should suggest ways in which students can make contact with English-language speakers. You should also assess whether the most effective way of improving language skills is to make friends with speakers of the language.

   Write your **article**.

3   An environmental organisation is inviting suggestions for new ways of raising people's awareness of the importance of protecting the countryside. You decide to write a letter in which you briefly describe your idea for a publicity campaign. You should also analyse the reasons why, in general, it is important to protect the countryside.

   Write your **letter**.

4   An English-language magazine called *Technology Today* is preparing a special edition on technological innovations of recent years such as new gadgets, applications for mobile phones or computer software. You decide to send in a review recommending something that you have found useful, briefly describing what it can do, and analysing the reasons why it has become popular.

   Write your **review**.

5   Write an answer to **one** of the following two questions based on **one** of the titles below. Write **5(a)** or **5(b)** at the beginning of your answer.

   (a)   Marc Norman and Tom Stoppard: *Shakespeare in Love*
         Your book group has asked for reports on screenplays to read in which minor characters play significant roles. You decide to write a report recommending *Shakespeare in Love* and briefly describing the roles played by three of the following: Kit (Christopher) Marlowe, the Queen, Webster and the Nurse. You should also assess any impact that these three characters had on Will or Viola.

         Write your **report**.

   (b)   Philip K Dick: *Do Androids Dream of Electric Sheep?*
         A student magazine is planning a series of articles called 'Future Visions', on some of the societies imagined by science fiction writers. You submit an article briefly describing the future world shown in *Do Androids Dream of Electric Sheep?*, and also explaining what people depend on for feelings of emotional satisfaction in this future world.

         Write your **article**.

LISTENING (40 minutes approximately)

Part 1

You will hear three different extracts. For questions **1–6**, choose the answer (**A**, **B** or **C**) which fits best according to what you hear.

There are two questions for each extract.

Extract One

You hear a science lecturer talking to students about the sense of taste.

1 How does the lecturer feel about the so-called 'Tongue Map'?

    A   surprised that it was accepted for so long
    B   frustrated by the diversity of views about it
    C   doubtful about whether it should continue to be used

2 Why does the lecturer refer to his own experience as a schoolchild?

    A   to encourage his students to trust their own judgement
    B   to show his students how scientific opinion changes over time
    C   to highlight the misleading nature of some classroom experiments

Extract Two

You hear a successful businessperson, Tom Meadon, talking about his career.

3 What does Tom say benefitted him most as a young man?

    A   the support of his family
    B   the decision to follow his own instincts
    C   the opportunities to travel to other countries

4 What is his attitude to Human Resources staff?

    A   He feels they have made some unwise changes.
    B   He is frustrated by their lack of commitment.
    C   He wishes they would be more open-minded.

Extract Three

You hear two students, Jacky and Martin, discussing power and influence.

5 What attribute do they agree gives one person most power over another?

    A   being intelligent
    B   possessing great wealth
    C   having an impressive job title

6 What has Jacky found out about people who are easily influenced?

    A   Their status in society has little impact.
    B   They frequently doubt their own abilities.
    C   Their gender is a significant factor.

Part 2

You will hear a sport psychologist called Brian Hawthorn giving a talk to psychology students about his profession.

For questions **7–15**, complete the sentences with a word or short phrase.

Brian says that sport psychologists assist both **(7)** .... and professional and amateur competitors.

Brian helps his clients deal with problems caused by **(8)** .... and emotional setbacks.

Brian says sport psychologists sometimes need to suggest ways for a trainer to improve **(9)** .... within their team.

Brian says most sport psychologists do **(10)** .... as well as private consultancy work.

According to Brian, all the techniques that sport psychologists use focus on encouraging **(11)** .... in their clients.

Brian refers to a **(12)** .... that people can make through visualisation before going to, for example, a job interview.

Brian suggests that a footballer failed because he was thinking about the **(13)** .... of his teammates.

Brian condemns the trend whereby a sportsman has **(14)** .... thrown at him from the crowd.

According to Brian, the ability to cope with **(15)** .... is what distinguishes the best sportspeople.

Part 3

You will hear a programme in which Rachel and Ian White talk about their office supplies company.

For questions **16–20**, choose the answer (**A, B, C** or **D**) which fits best according to what you hear.

16 How did the members of the Brisbane Business Network help Rachel and Ian?

    A   by suggesting possible sources of funding

    B   by giving them an idea of what was possible

    C   by advising them against expanding too fast

    D   by supporting them when they felt like giving up

17 What do Rachel and Ian say about choosing a website design company?

    A   Look at other websites they have made.

    B   Find out what qualifications and awards they have.

    C   Check that you can contact them later if you need to.

    D   Make sure they are already familiar with your type of business.

18 With regard to marketing, they recommend

    A   choosing techniques that require little time.

    B   checking that the database is regularly updated.

    C   making frequent visits to inform clients of developments.

    D   trying to build up a personal relationship with the client base.

19 When they asked for help with budgeting, they were relieved to find that

    A   their business was improving.

    B   they were doing better than their competitors.

    C   their accounts were becoming more accurate.

    D   their targets were appropriate.

20 Rachel and Ian found it useful to teach others about business plans because

    A   it reminded them of things they had forgotten.

    B   they got new ideas and insight from the students.

    C   it helped clarify things they had not understood before.

    D   they realised how much they had learned over the years.

Part 4

You will hear five short extracts in which university students are talking about a work placement that they did.

TASK ONE

For questions **21–25**, choose from the list (**A–H**) how each speaker found their work placement.

TASK TWO

For questions **26–30**, choose from the list (**A–H**) what each speaker found most useful during the work placement.

While you listen, you must complete both tasks.

A through a family member		
B on an academic website	Speaker 1	21
C through a chance meeting	Speaker 2	22
D on the Internet	Speaker 3	23
E at a university job fair	Speaker 4	24
F from a classmate's recommendation	Speaker 5	25
G through a contact in the sector		
H in a trade journal		

A getting to know colleagues		
B receiving feedback	Speaker 1	26
C doing work-based research	Speaker 2	27
D having to meet targets	Speaker 3	28
E getting used to a fixed routine	Speaker 4	29
F sharing opinions of proposals	Speaker 5	30
G putting theories into practice		
H being involved in basic procedures		

SPEAKING (16 minutes)

There are two examiners. One (the interlocutor) conducts the test, providing you with the necessary materials and explaining what you have to do. The other examiner (the assessor) will be introduced to you, but then takes no further part in the interaction.

Part 1 (2 minutes)

The interlocutor first asks you and your partner a few questions which focus on information about yourselves.

Part 2 (4 minutes)

In this part of the test you and your partner are asked to talk together. The interlocutor places a set of pictures on the table in front of you. There may be only one picture in the set or as many as seven pictures. This stimulus provides the basis for a discussion. The interlocutor first asks an introductory question which focuses on two of the pictures (or in the case of a single picture, on aspects of the picture). After about a minute, the interlocutor gives you both a decision-making task based on the same set of pictures.

The pictures for Part 2 are on pages C4–C5 of the colour section.

Part 3 (10 minutes)

You are each given the opportunity to talk for two minutes, to comment after your partner has spoken and to take part in a more general discussion.

The interlocutor gives you a card with a question written on it and asks you to talk about it for two minutes. After you have spoken, the interlocutor asks you both another question related to the topic on the card, addressing your partner first. This procedure is repeated, so that your partner receives a card and speaks for two minutes and a follow-up question is asked.

Finally, the interlocutor asks some further questions, which leads to a discussion on a general theme related to the subjects already covered in Part 3.

The cards for Part 3 are on pages C10–C11 of the colour section.

Test 3

READING AND USE OF ENGLISH (1 hour 30 minutes)

Part 1

For questions **1–8**, read the text below and decide which answer (**A, B, C** or **D**) best fits each gap.

Mark your answers **on the separate answer sheet**.

There is an example at the beginning (**0**).

0	**A**	bright	**B**	polished	**C**	shining	**D**	glossy

0	A	B	C	D

Nothing is impossible

Law firm Matthews and Reynolds is a **(0)** ..C... example of a business using art to revamp its public image. The firm hired an advertising agency called Eyeopener to carry out a rebranding **(1)** .... and gave the agency **(2)** .... rein to take the company by the scruff of the neck and effect a major makeover. The firm wanted smart, contemporary imagery which would symbolise an innovative, forward-thinking business.

(3) .... the firm now has a new logo, and all its advertising material features clever modern images which are **(4)** .... on the eye. Director Alan Ross comments: 'The images Eyeopener **(5)** .... say a lot about our approach, size and experience. And we were delighted with the advertising campaign they subsequently **(6)** ...., using a stylish, sophisticated approach with a touch of humour here and there.'

Public response to the rebranding has been excellent, and what appeared to be a **(7)** .... old law firm has been given a new lease of **(8)** .... as an adventurous and confident concern.

1 **A** routine   **B** exercise   **C** transaction   **D** function

2 **A** extra   **B** complete   **C** wide   **D** free

3 **A** In the end   **B** After all   **C** As a result   **D** In total

4 **A** easy   **B** attractive   **C** delightful   **D** agreeable

5 **A** stood up for   **B** came up with   **C** got through to   **D** fell back on

6 **A** portrayed   **B** devised   **C** imagined   **D** drafted

7 **A** dusty   **B** tedious   **C** murky   **D** monotonous

8 **A** fortune   **B** energy   **C** time   **D** life

Part 2

For questions **9–16**, read the text below and think of the word which best fits each space. Use only **one** word in each space. There is an example at the beginning **(0)**. Write your answers **IN CAPITAL LETTERS on the separate answer sheet**

Example: | **0** | T | O | | | | | | | | | | | | | | | | | | |

Neologisms – creating new words

To survive, language must evolve, yet it is resistant **(0)** ...<u>TO</u>.... certain forms of change. Most new words sparkle briefly, **(9)** .... at all, and then fade away. However, new words are necessary because, as the world changes, **(10)** .... must our vocabulary. In a society **(11)** .... science seems to occupy the intellectual high ground, it is inevitable that vocabularies are continually being augmented **(12)** .... technical terms.

Novel items of vocabulary distress people for two reasons. They attest to phenomena we don't like **(13)** .... expect not to like, and their tone offends our sensibilities. There is **(14)** .... new about this aversion to neologism. As far **(15)** .... as the 1750s, a distinguished English lexicographer criticised the 'unnecessary words creeping into the language'.

So what does make a word stick? First of all, it has to be widely adopted; it also has to denote something of lasting significance for it will only last as long as the phenomenon **(16)** .... question; and to become embedded, it needs to generate derivative forms.

Part 3

For questions **17–24**, read the text below. Use the word given in capitals at the end of some of the lines to form a word that fits in the space in the same line. There is an example at the beginning (**0**). Write your answers **IN CAPITAL LETTERS on the separate answer sheet**.

Example: | **0** | I | N | I | T | I | A | T | I | V | E | S | | | | | | |

Looking ahead to 2050

There are no guarantees as to what life will be like midway through the
21st century, but there are scientific (**0**) ..INITIATIVES.. which offer an interesting   **INITIATE**
glimpse into the future. Many people will work from home, electric cars will
be the typical form of transport, and goods and services paid for by mobile
phone. The most advanced smart homes will be (**17**) ....   **ENVIRONS**
friendly, equipped with their own (**18**) .... units which will be able   **CYCLE**
to make (**19**) .... waste water completely safe and palatable.   **DRINK**

Advances in medical science will also have far-reaching (**20**) .... ; people   **SEQUENCE**
born today can have a life (**21**) .... of 100 years. The development of   **EXPECT**
so-called smart medicine research suggests that people will carry out their
own digital health checks, enabling online analysts to reach an immediate
(**22**) .... of any condition requiring treatment.   **DIAGNOSE**

Scientists predict with reasonable (**23**) .... that some of these   **CERTAIN**
technological advances will be in place for many people worldwide, whereas the
nature of other changes remains (**24**) .... for the time being.   **SPECULATE**

Part 4

For questions **25–30**, complete the second sentence so that it has a similar meaning to the first sentence, using the word given **Do not change the word given.** You must use between **three** and **eight** words, including the word given. Here is an example (**0**).

Example:

0 Do you mind if I watch you while you paint?

objection

Do you .... you while you paint?

0	have any objection to my watching

Write **only** the missing words **on the separate answer sheet**.

---

25 Don't let Sarah's carefree attitude deceive you; she's an extremely conscientious worker.

taken

Don't let .... Sarah's carefree attitude; she's an extremely conscientious worker.

26 Fred didn't tell Sophie his news until she had finished her homework.

for

Fred .... telling her his news.

27 Although I am angry about what happened, in no circumstances would I want anyone to intervene on my behalf.

last

Although I am angry about what happened, the .... anyone to intervene on my behalf.

28   There is a rumour that the company lost over $20 million during the price war.

sustained

The company is rumoured .... over $20 million during the price war.

29   I ought to have had the roof repaired in the summer rather than leaving it until the autumn.

better

It .... had the roof repaired in the summer rather than leaving it until the autumn.

30   Alex made regular calls to his parents while travelling abroad.

kept

Alex .... his parents by phone while travelling abroad.

Part 5

You are going to read a newspaper article about libraries. For questions **31–36**, choose the answer
(**A**, **B**, **C** or **D**) which you think fits best according to the text. Mark your answers **on the separate
answer sheet**.

Why libraries matter in today's technological world

Municipal libraries are perhaps one of the most enduring public institutions – priceless repositories of history,
language, and culture. The dawn of the 'information superhighway' threatened to make them less relevant,
even obsolete. Yet now, these institutions are extending their mission well beyond the storage of knowledge.
Indeed, to distinguish themselves in a world where Google is well on its way to digitally scanning most of the
books ever written, libraries are learning to avail themselves of the simple fact that they are centrally located
in almost every community in the USA. In other words, libraries now see success being linked to their role as
public places and destinations.

While many US cities and towns now recognize the importance of re-inventing public libraries as
destinations, this awareness doesn't always translate into a well-rounded success. The most high-profile new
libraries rely on stylized designs to create buzz, feeding a false perception that public libraries are all about
attention-grabbing looks. But when the tour bus crowds stop coming, these libraries will sink or swim based
on how well they serve the needs of their respective communities – whether they are truly great places, not
just eye-catching buildings.

There are plenty of unsung libraries that embody a very different and more compelling vision of what it   *line 14*
means to be a public place. They may fly under the radar as architectural landmarks, but they still garner   *line 15*
respect, praise and even adoration on account of their innovative management and programming. They are
taking on a larger civic role – balancing their traditional needs and operations with outreach to the wider
community – thereby contributing to the creation of a physical commons that benefits the public as a whole.
If the traditional model of the library was the inward-focused community 'reading room', the current one is   *line 19*
more like a community 'front porch'.   *line 20*

But what of universities and other academic institutions; what is the value of an academic library in an age
of abundant information? A recent report commissioned by the Online Computer Library Center focusing on
college students found that they use libraries more than any other demographic group, that they like to help
themselves to information, that they are aware of the library's electronic resources, and that they identify
libraries with books (but they don't seem to feel that's a bad thing, unlike the so called experts who authored
the report who reveal deep dismay at that finding). What's more, they supplement library resources with ones
found on the web (no surprise there; don't we all?), they are largely satisfied with services and facilities and
they are strongly attached to the idea of libraries.

For college students, the library is like the poet Robert Frost's idea of home, 'the place where, when you
have to go there, they have to take you in.' They may not want to be there, they may not have any real curiosity
about the topic they are researching, but the library is a gateway to the sources they need, and for at least some
students the librarians are 'saviors' who help them take an assignment and locate sources that will match.

Of course, these days any distinction between library and digital information is obsolete. But there is a valid
distinction between printed book and the web, as there is between library and home computer. And the fact
is, there are things that the web cannot offer which any library can. In a library it's the totality of the experience
that matters: the website, the face-to-face services, the catalog, the collection. Staff are on hand to ensure
the user's reaction to the library is positive and productive, especially the novice user. Moreover, a library
creates relationships. It develops in users a sense of belonging, both to the library community, whether local
or academic, and to the wider world of knowledge. In this and other respects, the billions of web pages in
existence do not carry the same symbolic weight as the library. It stands for the importance of knowledge, for
access, for the idea that pursuing questions is a valuable human endeavor. We would do well not to dismiss
that symbolism as mere nostalgia.

31 What point is the writer making about public libraries in the first paragraph?

    A They are struggling to survive in the digital age.

    B They will have to find a completely new purpose.

    C They are taking full advantage of an existing benefit.

    D They may well have to give up their function of storing books.

32 In the second paragraph, the writer's purpose is to

    A warn libraries against trusting in new buildings to attract users.

    B praise libraries which recognize the benefits of tourism.

    C stress the need for libraries to consult local residents.

    D advise libraries to move to more central locations.

33 Which phrase illustrates 'a very different and more compelling vision of what it means to be a public place'? (lines 14–15)

    A they may fly under the radar (line 15)

    B architectural landmarks (line 15)

    C community 'reading room' (line 19)

    D community 'front porch' (line 20)

34 What is the writer emphasising in the first bracketed comment in the fourth paragraph?

    A her contempt for the reaction of the report writers

    B her concern for the outdated attitudes of the students

    C her doubt about the range of library users that were questioned

    D her distrust regarding the motives of those commissioning the report

35 Why does the writer quote the poet Robert Frost's definition of home?

    A to underline the literary value of a library's resources

    B to describe the function an academic library is required to fulfil

    C to suggest the paternal role taken by some college librarians

    D to express the sense of comfort libraries used to give their readers

36 In comparing libraries and the Internet, the writer

    A is urging libraries to concentrate on doing what they do best.

    B suggests there is no essential difference between them.

    C is making the case for the existence of libraries as a separate entity.

    D appears to regard libraries as an unnecessary luxury.

Part 6

You are going to read a magazine article about white-water rafting. Seven paragraphs have been removed from the extract. Choose from the paragraphs **A–H** the one which fits each gap (**37–43**). There is one extra paragraph which you do not need to use. Mark your answers **on the separate answer sheet**.

A Wet and Wonderful Ride

Cameron Wilson is swept away by the thrill of Tasmania's formidable Franklin River

Tasmania's Franklin River is a renowned rafting destination, both for the beauty and remoteness of the country through which it flows and for the challenge it presents the rafter. I'd been told by one of the guides on my trip that 'portage' is an indispensable word in the river rafter's lexicon. It derives from the French where it means 'physically carrying boats between two navigable stretches of a river'.

37

Such is the challenge of expedition rafting and the truth is, I was loving every minute of it. I glanced over at Brendan, at twenty-one the younger of our two river guides, and his grin confirmed that he too was having a ball, despite appearing in imminent danger of being swept off his feet and into the torrent. 'Mate,' he yelled over the roar of the rapids, 'like I keep telling them... this is not a holiday!'

38

A measure of respect, therefore, seemed in order, as I psyched myself up for rafting through the heart of the wilderness that had been so hard fought for. I was one of a group of ten – eight clients plus two guides – mustered over an early breakfast in Collingwood Bridge, two and a half hours north-west of the Tasmanian capital, Hobart.

39

A light drizzle was beginning to close in as we donned helmets and life-jackets, and pushed off into the gentle currents of a calm tributary. It was plain sailing so far, but I knew these tranquil waters would carry us on down to the raging Franklin. The afternoon was spent becoming acquainted with our raft buddies, or with pressing Shaun and Brendan for stories about Franklin expeditions from days gone by.

40

Thanks to the light but steady rain, however, the river level turned out to be high enough for us to glide over small rocks, and portage comfortably around the bigger ones, on the way to our first campsite. Conditions there turned out to be typical of those for the entire trip; the ravine drops steeply to the river and there is not much level ground, so rock overhangs make handy shelters.

41

The summit is more than half a vertical mile above the Franklin. It's the perfect spot from which to take in the unspoilt beauty of the country we'd been travelling through, its mountains, forests, high-country lakes and tarns.

42

Ironically enough, it was not until we struck one of the less celebrated stretches of white water that our only real rafting drama occurred. Shaun and his crew had wrapped their raft around a boulder and there it stayed for twenty minutes, held in place by the fast-flowing white water.

43

As the river widened, such white-knuckle experiences became fewer and further between, and as we eased into a leisurely paddling rhythm, twice I caught sight of platypus crossing the river. The silences grew longer and more comfortable, and as we slipped along under a blue sky the quiet was broken now and then by Shaun enquiring: 'How's the serenity?' On each occasion it was well above par.

A Having hung gamely on for a minute or two, Simon, a tax auditor from Brisbane, was finally dragged away for a bumpy solo ride to the bottom of the cascades. He came up bruised but smiling. I think it summed up how we were all feeling about the trip at that point.

B I had reason to reflect upon this information as I scrambled about on a slippery rock, trying to carry a heavy rubber raft between two boulders. The gap was too narrow and I was under constant assault from thousands of litres of white water. However expressed, this was a skill you couldn't do without if you were going to raft down the Franklin.

C It just went to prove how right our guide had been. A Franklin expedition is not a joy ride. It is, however, an opportunity to experience life on a river that, thanks to those who campaigned to save it, survives as one of the world's great wilderness journeys.

D Some of the stretches we'd be doing could be rafted straight through apparently, with the boulders under two metres of water. At other times the river gets so low we'd have to do a high portage – unload the gear, deflate and carry the lot through the forest. But you never knew because the river presents a new challenge each and every time.

E The moment arrived to pack our gear and supplies into barrels and 'dry bags' and lash these to aluminium frames, which were then secured in the two rafts. Our trip leader, Shaun, briefed us on how to handle a difficult portage or riding a rugged set of rapids, and talked us through ways of getting back into a raft from which you've just tumbled.

F The next few days saw both raft crews functioning superbly as we traversed the next section of river, responding as one to commands, as we bounced off logs and boulders through rapids. These were evocatively referred to by names such as 'The Cauldron', 'Nasty Notch' and 'Thunderush'.

G There was no doubting the truth of this assertion. I'd chosen this trip for a number of reasons, not least the fact that the Franklin is famous for the events of 1983. That's when thousands of people took to the streets or chained themselves to bulldozers to save it from being dammed and flooded, in what remains one of the largest environmental campaigns in Australia's history.

H Roused by Brendan, we'd be coaxed from our cocoons each day with the aroma of fresh coffee. On the day of our third such awakening, the sky had cleared beautifully, which meant fleece jackets and waterproofs could give way to dark glasses and sunscreen. The conditions were ideal for the long day's hike to Frenchman's Cap.

Part 7

You are going to read an article about ballet. For questions **44–53**, choose from the sections (**A–D**). The sections may be chosen more than once. Mark your answers **on the separate answer sheet.**

In which section does the writer mention

the level of fitness needed to engage in an activity?

| 44 | |

an explanation of the remedial health benefits of an activity?

| 45 | |

being surprised to see an outcome in a short space of time?

| 46 | |

ballet exercises as a form of escapism?

| 47 | |

a feeling of contentment arising out of physical activity?

| 48 | |

chance remarks that were a source of inspiration?

| 49 | |

the challenging range of skills and abilities required by ballet?

| 50 | |

the idea that people should attempt something beyond their normal capabilities?

| 51 | |

how an activity might be unfairly regarded by some people?

| 52 | |

the effect of the activity on the ability to resist an indulgence?

| 53 | |

Is ballet the new gym?

Celebrities are not alone in finding ballet training gives them a good workout, says Abigail Hoffman

A

I always find the winter months difficult here in London, but exercise can help to beat the winter blues because during any exercise routine, the body produces 'happy' endorphins. With attractive flushed cheeks and a warm glow of post-exercise smugness, you will feel much better than if you were suffering the inevitable side-effects of other types of weight-loss programme. I'm not suggesting you high-tail it to the gym, however. Gyms are anathema to many, who perceive them as overly competitive and so twentieth century. No, I'm recommending that you follow the example of celebrities and take to the barre. Devotees in New York, London and Paris cite suppleness, strength and a sculpted silhouette as the chief benefits of a ballet-based fitness regime. Deride it, if you will, as the latest media-fuelled fad, but increasingly exercise professionals are referring to ballet as the 'new Pilates'. Its benefits have also been noted by the New Zealand rugby team, who have been known to incorporate ballet moves into their training routine.

B

Charlotte Toner, a former professional ballerina, has been at the forefront of this trend. Some years ago, she developed what is known as her 'floor barre' class, which incorporates elementary ballet and Pilates-type movements. 'I fell into teaching it because my friends were always asking how I kept in shape,' she says. 'Then I discovered there was so much demand that I had to get my act together and produce a proper timetable.' Injured dancers often do floor barre because as the name implies, you work mainly lying on the floor rather than standing at the barre. Since the back is supported, it's relatively risk-free. Joy Waiter, a leading physiotherapist, says: 'This combination of movement and stretch, underpinned by stability, is a good model for most people with back problems. Floor barre is also an ideal exercise routine for those not in the first flush of youth.' Ballet's focus on lengthening rather than contracting muscles promotes flexibility, maintaining a lithe appearance. 'If you attend class regularly, you'll be noticing a difference in body shape in no time,' Charlotte assured me.

C

Charlotte offers a variety of classes, each lasting seventy-five minutes, and can accommodate complete beginners at floor barre as well as advanced ballet performers. Participants span the generations and it's comforting to realise that you don't need the co-ordination skills of an acrobat or the stamina of an Olympic marathon runner to attempt a plié at the barre. 'If you can walk on a treadmill,' she insists, 'you can do floor barre.' Co-ordination, elegance and suppleness come with practice. I was recommended to take up floor barre when persistent lower back pain prevented me from working out in the gym. After a mere six-week course with Charlotte, attending three sessions a week, my back improved and muscle tone was starting to replace dimpled flab. I also lost 4.5kg effortlessly; somehow glimpsing my podgy reflection in triplicate in the studio mirrors eviscerated my desire for chips and chocolate.

D

But the appeal goes beyond the visible results; many devotees highlight another side of ballet. 'It's about expressing myself in a different way,' one says. 'The melodic music transports you far from the daily grind.' Françoise Peretti, managing director of her own public-relations firm, puts it well. 'Ballet tones my body but it also tones my soul,' she says. 'As a former investment banker used to analysing the nuances of financial markets, I was unprepared for how ballet challenges the intellect as well as the body. There's a litany of things to remember and it calls for both concentration and mental agility. Co-ordinating your arms and legs is difficult enough but you also have to simultaneously stand tall, lower your shoulders, breathe correctly and memorise the often complex routines.' So, if you too are gazing despondently at the overcast sky, wondering desperately how you're ever going to get through the winter months as you long to burrow back under the bedcovers, think about shaking a leg – literally. Step outside your comfort zone and treat yourself to a fitness regime that is fun, uplifting and very effective. Take up floor barre. Your thighs will thank you for it.

WRITING (1 hours 30 minutes)

Part 1

Read the two texts below.

Write an essay summarising and evaluating the key points from both texts. Use your own words throughout as far as possible, and include your own ideas in your answers.

Write your answer in **240–280** words.

1

Eating together

It is often said that a pleasure shared is a pleasure doubled, and who can deny that conversation around the dinner table provides opportunities for a family or friends to share their happiness, express their feelings and learn from one another. Meals taken together foster warmth, security and love, as well as feelings of belonging. This unifying role that food can play in our lives can be seen on a much bigger scale, too. Many cultures have rich culinary traditions, and the distinctiveness or the quality of their food can be a powerful source of pride, strengthening a sense of cultural or national identity.

Food, glorious food!

In today's undeniably stressful, fast-moving world, the increasing popularity of convenience food should come as no surprise. Despite warnings from doctors about the possible health risks of such food, it is all too easy to pop something in the microwave every day, and in so doing miss out on one of life's great experiences, which is cooking fresh food. Not only does preparing home-made food give satisfaction, and the results taste immeasurably better than the tinned or packaged variety, but, more significantly, it gives the opportunity to display care and affection through hospitality shown to guests.

Write your **essay**.

Part 2

Write an answer to **one** of the questions 2–5 in this part. Write your answer in **280–320** words in an appropriate style.

2   Your college magazine has asked its readers to send in reviews of the leisure opportunities available in the nearby town. You decide to submit a review of a sports centre in town. In your review you should briefly describe the facilities available, and assess the extent to which you consider that it meets the needs of the students.

Write your **review**.

3   An international magazine is planning a feature on the importance of understanding the past. You decide to write a letter in which you briefly describe an important event in your country's history which you think everybody ought to be aware of. You should also explain the extent to which we can ever understand the present without knowing about the past.

Write your **letter**.

4   An English-language newspaper is inviting readers to contribute to a series of articles about interesting possessions that have been handed down to them by family members. You decide to write an article about something you have inherited from a family member. You should describe what it is and explain why, in general, you think it is important to pass on interesting possessions to future generations.

Write your **article**.

5   Write an answer to **one** of the following two questions based on **one** of the titles below. Write **5(a)** or **5(b)** at the beginning of your answer.

(a)   Marc Norman and Tom Stoppard: *Shakespeare in Love*
       An English-language newspaper has invited readers to send in reviews of screenplays based on the theme of mistaken identities and the misunderstandings that result. You decide to submit a review of *Shakespeare In Love*. Your review should briefly describe how different characters mislead one another, explain why they do so and consider whether their behaviour has any serious consequences.

Write your **review**.

(b)   Philip K Dick: *Do Androids Dream of Electric Sheep?*
       You have been studying *Do Androids Dream of Electric Sheep?* in your English language lessons, and your tutor has asked you to write an essay on bounty hunters. In your essay, you should briefly describe the characters of Rick Deckard and Phil Resch and the work they do, and assess the extent to which you think their attitudes to their job change in the course of the novel.

Write your **essay**.

LISTENING (40 minutes approximately)

Part 1

You will hear three different extracts.

For questions **1–6**, choose the answer (**A**, **B** or **C**) which fits best according to what you hear.

There are two questions for each extract.

Extract One

You hear an art gallery guide talking about the paintings of Marianne North, a nineteenth-century traveller and botanical artist.

1 The guide suggests that Marianne North's work is important

   A   as historical documentation.
   B   for its range of subject matter.
   C   because of technical expertise.

2 The guide refers to a change in people's attitude towards

   A   the role of education.
   B   the value of artistic skills.
   C   the relationships between men and women.

Extract Two

You hear part of an interview with Professor Renton, who has recently been appointed director of a science museum.

3 What does Professor Renton suggest that he has inherited?

   A   his enquiring mind
   B   his problem-solving skills
   C   his talent for gathering facts

4 Professor Renton says that one of the museum's aims should be to

   A   reassure visitors about current issues.
   B   enable visitors to draw conclusions.
   C   interpret evidence for visitors.

Extract Three

You hear an economist talking about technological developments.

5 What is his attitude towards the Internet?

    A   Its practical drawbacks have been overemphasised.
    B   Its effects on business have generally been exaggerated.
    C   Its social importance has been overestimated by entrepreneurs.

6 What does he say about washing machines?

    A   They led to an expansion of the labour market.
    B   They were initially only available to wealthier people.
    C   They were an early sign of changing attitudes to women.

Part 2

You will hear part of a lecture about ancient Egyptian ships and an attempt to reconstruct one. For questions **7–15**, complete the sentences with a word or short phrase.

Archaeologists believe that the site called Mersa Gawasis was once a
(7) .... on the Red Sea.

To gain the support from the **(8)** ...., the Pharaoh Hatshepsut
imported incense by ship.

Ancient Egyptian shipbuilders differed from modern ones in that they did not make a
(9) .... for the ship they were building.

The speaker compares building an ancient Egyptian ship to doing a
(10) ....

The Egyptian river ship used **(11)** .... to help attach planks
together, unlike the seagoing ships.

Wood from trees grown in **(12)** .... was used in the reconstruction
of the ship.

The modern shipbuilders were provided with a **(13)** ....
by the archaeologists.

The modern shipbuilders used **(14)** .... to make the ship watertight.

The modern team used a **(15)** .... to get the ship to the sea.

Part 3

You will hear two costume design students, Angela and Mike, discussing the role of costumes in films.

For questions **16–20**, choose the answer (**A**, **B**, **C** or **D**) which fits best according to what you hear.

16 At the beginning of their course, they were asked to watch a film with the sound turned off to see if they could

    A still follow the details of the plot.
    B spot small inconsistencies in costumes.
    C identify the main themes of the film.
    D predict the development of characters' relationships.

17 Which aspect of the course particularly interests Mike?

    A the importance of film as social history
    B the way film influences fashion
    C costume-making techniques
    D the sourcing of fashion accessories

18 What interpretation of a female character wearing layers of clothes do they find implausible?

    A that she is shy and lacks confidence
    B that she has a complex personality
    C that she wants to hide her past
    D that she is still searching for her true identity

19 What compromise do they agree costume designers have to make?

    A They have to sacrifice authenticity for dramatic effect.
    B They have to make costumes that are comfortable for actors to wear.
    C They substitute poorer-quality fabrics because of budget constraints.
    D They carry out limited research because of tight deadlines.

20 What is Angela going to do her next project on?

    A how to make costumes for films with large numbers of minor characters
    B how to alter costumes to reflect the development of the main character
    C how the significance of items of clothing has changed over time
    D how male film-makers have misunderstood the role of women

Part 4

You will hear five short extracts in which people are talking about their experiences in their first jobs.

TASK ONE

For questions **21–25**, choose from the list (**A–H**) what skill each speaker developed during their first job.

TASK TWO

For questions **26–30**, choose from the list (**A–H**) what each speaker appreciated most in their first job.

While you listen, you must complete both tasks.

A translating

B time management

C giving presentations

D financial planning

E giving feedback

F interpreting data

G problem solving

H delegating tasks

Speaker 1	21
Speaker 2	22
Speaker 3	23
Speaker 4	24
Speaker 5	25

A the friendliness of colleagues

B flexible working hours

C out-of-work activities

D hands-on learning style

E the opportunity to deal with a challenge

F travel opportunities

G financial incentives

H promotion opportunity

Speaker 1	26
Speaker 2	27
Speaker 3	28
Speaker 4	29
Speaker 5	30

SPEAKING (16 minutes)

There are two examiners. One (the interlocutor) conducts the test, providing you with the necessary materials and explaining what you have to do. The other examiner (the assessor) will be introduced to you, but then takes no further part in the interaction.

Part 1 (2 minutes)

The interlocutor first asks you and your partner a few questions which focus on information about yourselves.

Part 2 (4 minutes)

In this part of the test you and your partner are asked to talk together. The interlocutor places a set of pictures on the table in front of you. There may be only one picture in the set or as many as seven pictures. This stimulus provides the basis for a discussion. The interlocutor first asks an introductory question which focuses on two of the pictures (or in the case of a single picture, on aspects of the picture). After about a minute, the interlocutor gives you both a decision-making task based on the same set of pictures.

The pictures for Part 2 are on pages C6–C7 of the colour section.

Part 3 (10 minutes)

You are each given the opportunity to talk for two minutes, to comment after your partner has spoken and to take part in a more general discussion.

The interlocutor gives you a card with a question written on it and asks you to talk about it for two minutes. After you have spoken, the interlocutor asks you both another question related to the topic on the card, addressing your partner first. This procedure is repeated, so that your partner receives a card and speaks for two minutes and a follow-up question is asked.

Finally, the interlocutor asks some further questions, which leads to a discussion on a general theme related to the subjects already covered in Part 3.

The cards for Part 3 are on pages C10–C11 of the colour section.

Test 4

READING AND USE OF ENGLISH (1 hour 30 minutes)

Part 1

For questions **1–8**, read the text below and decide which answer (**A**, **B**, **C** or **D**) best fits each gap.

Mark your answers **on the separate answer sheet**.

There is an example at the beginning (**0**).

| 0 | **A** | managed | **B** | functioned | **C** | performed | **D** | worked |

0	A	B	C	D

Photography at its most daring

Photographers who have (**0**) ....D..... so close to volcanoes that their clothes started to burn, come within stroking (**1**) .... of tigers in the wild, or dived under sea ice in freezing cold water have (**2**) .... forces for an exhibition, (**3**) .... as displaying images from the harshest places on Earth

Polar bears and seals were (**4**) .... on camera by a photographer who grew up in the Arctic and trained as a (**5**) .... biologist. He dives under sea ice to swim with his subjects, once offending a leopard seal by (**6**) .... the penguin she tried to feed him with. Another exhibitor has recorded not only tigers but also chimpanzees that had never before encountered human beings. The volcano enthusiasts work in fireproof suits, always at risk of becoming so (**7**) .... by the beauty of the eruptions that they venture too close. There are invisible pockets of gas as well as flames, all of which contribute to the (**8**) .... perils of being an extreme photographer.

1 **A** interval **B** space **C** distance **D** reach

2 **A** united **B** joined **C** merged **D** integrated

3 **A** billed **B** announced **C** labelled **D** scheduled

4 **A** snatched **B** captured **C** taken **D** suspended

5 **A** aquatic **B** sea **C** marine **D** ocean

6 **A** repulsing **B** denying **C** dismissing **D** refusing

7 **A** transfixed **B** bound **C** focussed **D** held

8 **A** reckless **B** deadly **C** alarming **D** fearful

Part 2

For questions **9–16**, read the text below and think of the word which best fits each space. Use only one word in each space. There is an example at the beginning (**0**). Write your answers **IN CAPITAL LETTERS on the separate answer sheet**.

Example: | 0 | A | M | O | U | N | T | | | | | | | | | | | |

Altering the modern mind

A recently published book claims that the **(0)** A̲M̲O̲U̲N̲T̲. of time we spend on the Internet is changing the very structure of our brains. Its thesis is simple enough: not only that the modern world's relentless informational overload is killing our capacity **(9)** ………. reflection, contemplation and patience, but that our online habits are also altering the way our brains are wired.

In the book, the author looks **(10)** ………. on such human inventions as the map and the clock and the **(11)** ………. to which they influenced our essential models of thought. He argues that the Internet's multiplicity of stimuli and mass of information have **(12)** ………. rise to hurried and distracted thinking. Without putting too fine a point on it, the author concludes that our ability to learn **(13)** ………. at all worthwhile has become superficial. Surprisingly very **(14)** ………. research has looked into the Internet's effects on the brain, but further research is **(15)** ………. hand and is investigating whether deep-thinking processes really are in **(16)** ………. of disappearing.

Part 3

For questions **17–24**, read the text below. Use the word given in capitals at the end of some of the lines to form a word that fits in the space in the same line. There is an example at the beginning (**0**). Write your answers **IN CAPITAL LETTERS on the separate answer sheet**.

Example: | **0** | G | L | O | B | A | L | | | | | | | | | | | |

Windfarms

Windfarms are hailed as powerful weapons in the battle against (**0**) ...GLOBAL... warming; it is considered by many to be politically incorrect to criticise them. They are clean, green and therefore (**17**) ...., and viewed as such throughout the world. There is a **GLOBE**

VIRTUE

(**18**) .... to wind turbines, of course. **SIDE**
They are enormous and dominate the landscape; they make a noise that condemns people to (**19**) .... nights. One turbine standing alone in a windswept setting could be described as beautiful, but can the same description be applied to a whole host of them? But all these drawbacks pale into (**20**) ...., we are told, compared to the great benefits that will result from this renewable energy source. **SLEEP**

SIGNIFY

However, there is as yet no economic way of storing electricity; turbines generate it only when the wind blows, not (**21**) .... when demand is high; (**22**) .... of carbon from the plants manufacturing turbines are considerable. (**23**) ...., the environmental pollution caused by the extraction of a metal crucial to their construction is potentially (**24**) .... **NECESSARY**

EMIT

ADD

DISASTER

Part 4

For questions **25–30**, complete the second sentence so that it has a similar meaning to the first sentence, using the word given. **Do not change the word given.** You must use between **three** and **eight** words, including the word given. Here is an example (**0**).

Example:

0 Do you mind if I watch you while you paint?

objection

Do you .... you while you paint?

0	have any objection to my watching

Write **only** the missing words **on the separate answer sheet**.

---

25 Unless Sam's plans change over the weekend, we'll leave early on Monday morning.

no

Providing .... over the weekend, we'll leave early on Monday morning.

26 As far as I know, Simon will be here on Thursday.

suppose

I've .... be here on Thursday.

27 The role played by the PR company in securing the government contract was never acknowledged officially.

official

At no time .... the role the PR company played securing the government contract.

28 Passengers are absolutely forbidden to cross the railway track.

account

On .... to cross the railway track.

29 I have no idea why my email bounced back.

loss

I .... why my email bounced back.

30 Felix doesn't intend to make the same mistake again.

no

Felix .... the same mistake again.

Part 5

You are going to read a newspaper article about people's attitudes to their possessions in a digital age. For questions **31–36**, choose the answer (**A, B, C** or **D**) which you think fits best according to the text. Mark your answers **on the separate answer sheet**.

Less is More

How do people cut down on their possessions in a digital age

The 17th century French artist Poussin is well-known for his paintings, usually set in serene and idyllic pastoral landscapes, which convey serious lessons for mankind. These messages are sometimes a bit obscure, and some continue to puzzle art historians, but in the picture *Landscape with Diogenes*, things seem relatively straightforward. The ancient philosopher Diogenes is depicted casting away his last possession, a drinking bowl. He realises he doesn't need it after seeing a youth cupping a hand to drink from a river. The significance for us is that Diogenes' spiritual descendants known as 'new minimalists' are now everywhere, if not as radically possession-free as he was.

There are hundreds of websites extolling the virtues of uncluttered living. 'I can carry everything I own,' says Kevin. 'I have a few changes of clothing, laptop, two pots, bowl, spoon, fork, futon and flask. I like sitting on the floor eating fruit, nuts, vegetables and rice.' At this point I really hated Kevin, but I should have known better because he continued, 'The nice thing about a bare room is that you begin to notice other things like the changing sunlight during the day. Many possessions tend to tie one down mentally and physically – seeing too much permanence in inanimate objects rather than being aware of the vitality of the outside world of nature.'

Everyone is trying to cut down on things these days. People are trying to reduce their carbon footprints, their waistlines, their monthly outgoings. What's more, there's a general fear that people are becoming asphyxiated by their possessions, and this is fuelled by the knowledge that, according to innumerable sociological surveys, the leading pastime these days seems to be shopping. It's true, sales of e-readers and e-books outstrip those of paperbacks, and we know that only losers and reactionaries buy camera film today. As a result, the need for bookshelves and photo albums is cut out.

However, today's new minimalists don't urge us to burn our books and crush our CDs, but just make sure we have them as digital files. So, for example, I have digitised versions of some of my old vinyl LP records and haven't, as yet, stirred myself to take the LPs to the nearest charity shop – and I admit I shall probably go on keeping them. Technology has, perhaps, gone beyond our dreams and there is always the lurking suspicion that our hard drives will crash and all will be lost. Far more important, however, is the fact that our memories are so inextricably tied to our possessions that we can't get rid of stuff. No matter how much glossy magazines insist that we should.

We are not exactly suffering withdrawal symptoms as we try to break our addiction to objects. We are just acquiring new stuff that means we can bin or recycle our old stuff. Diogenes, who was quite the cynic philosopher, would have seen through this imposture in seconds. Those who can afford to, buy the kit to make the minimalist dream a reality, but they are still investing in commodities, just different ones from those they collected a decade earlier.

A few years ago I wrote a piece predicting the demise of incredibly expensive watches, believing that they would inevitably be eclipsed by the amazingly more versatile mobile phone, no matter how beautifully crafted and elegant they might be, but they still seem to be covetable objects of conspicuous consumption. Clearly the ostensible function of a £20k watch is negligible enticement to owning it. Here then is another manifestation of the lure of possessions – we are not only sentimental in our attachment to them, but also status driven.

I'm happy to have found another website which seems to solve a whole lot of problems at once – a thriving online advice surgery offering storage solutions. The interior designer responsible for this does not counsel getting rid of stuff, but rather recommends buying more stuff (elegant flexible trugs, colourful lidded containers) to hide the first lot of stuff from view. I love this philosophy – get that decluttered minimalist look, convince yourself you've got your desire for possessions under control, without having to lose a thing. There's no reason to think such bad faith will change soon: we aren't ruthless enough to emulate Diogenes and cast away all our possessions.

31 Why does the writer refer to a painting by the artist Poussin?

- **A** Its message is not as simple as it appears.
- **B** Its meaning is only now becoming clear.
- **C** It illustrates a very modern trend.
- **D** It portrays a very wise philosopher.

32 What lesson did the writer take from his own reaction to Kevin's blog?

- **A** Learn to enjoy your natural surroundings.
- **B** Don't be too quick to judge people.
- **C** Take pleasure in the simple things of life.
- **D** Don't become tied down by possessions.

33 In the writer's opinion, what prompts people to want to reduce their possessions?

- **A** unease about the acquisitive nature of modern society
- **B** a desire to take advantage of new technology
- **C** a concern about wasting money
- **D** an urge to simplify their lives

34 The writer thinks minimalism will not succeed in the long term because of people's

- **A** lack of faith in digital hardware.
- **B** laziness in the face of change.
- **C** nostalgia for physical objects.
- **D** resistance to media pressure.

35 The writer suggests Diogenes would have viewed modern attempts at minimalism with

- **A** indifference.
- **B** sympathy.
- **C** approval.
- **D** contempt.

36 According to the writer, people invest in smart new storage in order to

- **A** ease their conscience over having too many things.
- **B** provide a temporary solution to a problem.
- **C** make attractive additions to their homes.
- **D** indulge their desire to make purchases.

Part 6

You are going to read a newspaper article about psychology. Seven paragraphs have been removed from the extract. Choose from the paragraphs **A–H** the one which fits each gap (**37–43**). There is one extra paragraph which you do not need to use. Mark your answers **on the separate answer sheet**.

Psychology: just common sense?

For many sceptics, it was a sweet moment when, at a recent science meeting, a psychology professor denounced his own discipline as 'banal' and 'a fake science'. As a rehearsal for an international conference on the theme of 'critical psychology', Professor Ian Parker was addressing the British Psychology Association.

| 37 | |

So it was a relief for some to hear of Professor Parker's claim that psychologists 'don't tell us anything we don't already know'. The rebel professor argues that psychology cannot claim to be a science because it is unable to subject itself to the same research and validation processes that biology, physics and chemistry do. This accusation has been made loudly for decades and he says the subject has done little to improve itself. 'Psychology pretends to be a science but it is not a science and it is questionable whether it could ever be one,' he says.

| 38 | |

For a long time, psychologists have attempted to address the issue of what effect this attitude has. Some have incorporated into their conclusions the influence it has on results, exposing it instead of making ineffectual attempts to hide it. And new, more sophisticated theories have arisen. Professor Parker thinks a few of these have been useful but most are merely fads: 'They are there for about 10 years and then they disappear.'

| 39 | |

Professor Parker accepts that these may be cheap experiment fodder. But, he argues, how many of us feel that their behaviour yields much insight into the rest of us? In some institutions, he claims, it is now becoming compulsory for them to take part in psychology experiments, narrowing even further the range of people that is studied.

| 40 | |

Thus, the psychologist who studies, say, impulse buying, must first test our preconceptions about the habit to decide on common views on it. After that, he then makes more detailed investigations to see if the evidence supports them. In this way, psychologists' conclusions would be supported by layer upon layer of reliable evidence.

| 41 | |

A key problem here is that humans themselves keep changing, partly in response to what psychologists have previously told them about themselves. Ask the man on the street to account for his behaviour and he may well invoke his 'unconscious' in the explanation. But before the concept of the unconscious was invented by Freud, the man would have explained himself differently.

| 42 | |

The fact that fashions in psychology can change so dramatically is one more argument in Professor Parker's attack on his own profession. But whatever doubts he and those who support him hold, there is no denying the great public and media appetite for the results of even the smallest of experiments conducted by the most inexperienced of researchers.

| 43 | |

There is a willing audience ready to absorb and believe things that affect all of us in our daily lives. And so without challenge, without counter-proposition, yet another rumour would enter the world of popular psychology, masquerading as proven fact.

A Although he therefore acknowledges that there have been some positive developments, Professor Parker believes there are still some very obvious problems with psychologists' techniques. An example is the temptation among university researchers to study only undergraduates.

B Psychological theories even cause people to behave differently. The agony aunts advising people on their problems in British newspapers and magazines fifty years ago absorbed the psychology of their generation and urged readers to repress feelings which they would now encourage them to indulge.

C Moreover, it is testimony to psychology's success that much of its research now appears common sense. This is because psychology's findings are more generally disseminated to a general audience than other sciences. But why is this the case?

D The week-long get-together was packed with interesting science but some of the psychology presentations were so dubious that delegates were already inclining towards his views. One researcher, for example, had discovered that impulse buyers like clothes and hi-fis but are not tempted by gardening tools or car equipment.

E But this is what Professor Parker thinks is missing: 'If the theories are built up on solid ground, the question is: where is the building? The magnificent tower of psychological knowledge never appears,' he says.

F As a result, just a day's research by a student has in the past been deemed worthy of presentation at a psychology conference. It has then duly been reported by uncritical newspapers.

G One contributing factor to this lack of academic rigour, he believes, is that the subjects who volunteer for psychology experiments are different from the rest of us. Investigations have shown that they are more insecure and they try harder to please. Indeed, they try hard to discover what result the researcher wants and then help to produce it.

H Combine this with the 'banal' or 'common sense' results that seem to flood psychology journals and conferences, and it is not surprising that the discipline of psychology may appear ridiculous to some outsiders. To restore its reputation, first and foremost psychologists must establish the foundations of their research to avoid creating a structure that rests on mere hearsay.

Part 7

You are going to read a newspaper article about poetry. For questions **44–53**, choose from the sections (**A–D**). The sections may be chosen more than once. Mark your answers **on the separate answer sheet**.

In which section does the writer mention

the possibility of a poem following certain conventions?	44
poetry which sounds like prose?	45
particular lines of poems being precious to most people?	46
poetry being instantly recognisable?	47
evidence that poetry has long been seen as a creative act?	48
poetry being the ultimate expression of an intellectual mind?	49
professional respect for the integrity of poetry?	50
the possibility of poetry dealing with everyday matters?	51
poetry's relative lack of exposure?	52
poetry that relies for its effectiveness purely on its emotional resonance?	53

Poetry

The writer AA Gill reflects on the nature of poetry

A

One of the most satisfying things about words is their black and whiteness, the neat, austere simplicity of their process. Letters on a page are so direct and literal; you read a sentence and you can trace the thought. You know how it's done – just so long as it's prose. With poetry, however, the rules don't apply. On the face of it, it looks the same; the letters, the words, are familiar. But by some internal magic, poetry hovers above the page. It happens outside the black and white lines. Poetry is in essence a mysterious art. Poems are coded messages for your eyes only, left under pillows, tied to roses, written in water. There are no regular poetry reviews in cultural magazines, or poetry programmes on the telly. I expect Seamus Heaney and Wendy Cope could stroll hand in hand through most bookshops unmolested. Poems sell few and far, for little or less. But this reticence belies the truth of verse. Even if we haven't read a new poem for a decade, still there are verses that are the most dear cultural amulets we own, hidden in the dead letterboxes of our hearts. Snatches of verse, we take them to our end.

B

I write about 1,500 words every day. I handle them with respect and pleasure, for they are the tools of my trade. I reckon I can make a craftsman-like job of most wordy things, from a shopping list to a eulogy. But I have no idea, not the faintest inkling, of how a poem is made, and not for want of trying. Of course, I've tried. I've chopped the lines out, I've counted the syllables and made similes and metaphors, but it's barely poetry. It remains resolutely page-bound: prosaic, poetish pastiche. The hardest thing after writing poetry is writing about poetry, as you must already have noticed. It makes the author sound either pretentiously airy-fairy or thuggishly indifferent. For a start, nobody has really even satisfactorily defined what poetry is. Have a look in any dictionary, and you'll see what I mean. The word 'poet' got its first recorded use in English in the 14th century. It came from the Ancient Greek for 'the maker'. People have written books defining what poetry is and isn't, but they can only tell you the mechanics. I asked an editor what poetry was. She said, 'It's that which can't be edited.'

C

You know poetry the moment you see it; the first line tells you. Yet it has no rules. It can rhyme or not. It can have as many rhythms as a Brazilian ballroom, lines of any length, as much or as little punctuation as it feels like. But poetry can also be as rigorous as mathematics. It exists outside grammar and formula, and yet it can tie itself up in manners and etiquette. It can have any number of subtly different meanings; indeed, it can have no logical meaning at all, yet still be beautiful and touching and disturbing. A woman once wrote to Dylan Thomas saying that she loved his poetry, but was worried that her understanding of it was not what he'd intended. Thomas replied that a poem was like a city: it had many entrances.

D

I have yet to hear a convincing explanation of where poetry comes from and how it arrives, but I do know it is the highest calling of a sensitive and cerebral existence. Poetry, along with dancing and drumming is probably the most ancient of all our arts. There was rhythm and rhyme before written language. Poems lit up the memory of our collective past, told us who we were and where we came from, and they still do. People who never read poetry still reach for it at the precipitous points of their existence. At times of great happiness or terrible sadness, those places where prose is leaden with its own wordiness, only poetry will do. And there is poetry for every occasion. In my life we have had a particularly rich period of poets: Auden, Graves, Larkin, Thomas, Betjeman, to name but five. They have written between the lines on every facet of our lives, from sport to table manners. The poetry of our times is a fairer record of our concerns and hopes and our collective life than film or television or painting.

WRITING (1 hours 30 minutes)

Part 1

Read the two texts below.

Write an essay summarising and evaluating the key points from both texts. Use your own words throughout as far as possible, and include your own ideas in your answers.

Write your answer in **240–280** words.

1

Reading Habits

For many young adults embarking on their university or college courses, reading can stop being fun and become a chore. Faced with piles of compulsory reading, it is no surprise that it loses its appeal. It is such a pity because when they were children, reading was an enormous source of pleasure, stimulating their imaginations and widening their horizons. Science fiction novels could open up the possibility of a future as a brilliant scientist, adventure stories of a dreamed-of life as an intrepid explorer. Children's choice of books often reveal their developing personalities.

Reading Aloud

Much of the pleasure of reading lies in sharing your reactions with others. I personally believe that reading aloud is a perfect pastime for all ages whether it be to a child at bedtime or an overworked and stressed adult. Listening to the written word on the radio or as a member of a book group in the company of others and discussing what you have heard is a rewarding and exhilarating experience. It allows individuals to find meaning together, to make connections and uncover memories. To put it briefly, it makes the world a better place.

Write your **essay**.

Part 2

Write an answer to **one** of the questions **2–5** in this part. Write your answer in **280–320** words in an appropriate style.

---

2 An international travel organisation is publishing a book entitled *Travel Changes Lives* and has asked for contributions. You decide to submit an article about a travel experience that has changed your life. You should briefly describe the experience, explain what made it so special and assess the significance of the changes in your life as a result.

Write your **article**.

3 An English-language magazine called *International Sport* is inviting readers to write in with the name of either an individual or a team who deserve recognition for a great achievement in international sport. You decide to write a letter to the magazine with your suggestion briefly describing what was achieved, and assessing how difficult it was for the individual or team to achieve their success.

Write your **letter**.

4 An international leisure magazine is running a series on comedy programmes shown on television around the world. It has asked readers to send in reports on comedy programmes in their countries. You decide to send in a report on a television comedy programme from your country in which you briefly describe the programme. You should also explain what it is about the characters in the programme that makes the comedy appeal to many people in your country.

Write your **report**.

5 Write an answer to **one** of the following two questions based on **one** of the titles below. Write **5(a)** or **5(b)** at the beginning of your answer

(a) Marc Norman and Tom Stoppard: *Shakespeare in Love*
A magazine has published a feature about the theme of marriage in literature. You decide to write a letter to the magazine about *Shakespeare in Love*, comparing Viola's relationships with Will and Wessex. You should also explain why Viola marries Wessex and cannot marry Will.

Write your **letter**.

(b) Philip K Dick: *Do Androids Dream of Electric Sheep?*
Your student magazine has asked for reviews of science-fiction novels. You decide to submit a review of *Do Androids Dream of Electric Sheep?* Your review should briefly explain the themes of love and loneliness in the novel with reference to Rick Deckard and John Isidore, and assess whether it is the treatment of these themes that makes the book worth reading.

Write your **review**.

LISTENING (40 minutes approximately)

Part 1

You will hear three different extracts.

For questions **1–6**, choose the answer (**A**, **B** or **C**) which fits best according to what you hear.

There are two questions for each extract.

___

Extract One

You hear Sarah Carpenter being interviewed about a campaign called Online Now, which aims to give more people in Britain access to computers.

1 Why does Sarah say she wants to increase internet use so urgently?

    A   to improve international communication
    B   to prevent an increase in social inequality
    C   to involve people in economic development

2 How does Sarah say increased computer use should be achieved?

    A   by improved access to existing facilities
    B   by increased investment in education
    C   by government subsidies for community centres

Extract Two

You hear a museum curator talking about one exhibit, a pestle, which was used for grinding food.

3 What does he say about the handle of the pestle?

    A   It may originally have been designed for another purpose.
    B   It was probably made after the ball of the pestle.
    C   Its form is unrelated to its intended function.

4 According to the curator, what was striking about the first plants cultivated by humans?

    A   They were all varieties of wild grasses.
    B   They were all inedible in their natural state.
    C   They all formed part of the diet of other animals.

Extract Three

You hear a marine biologist talking about measures to protect the oceans from pollution.

5 Why has protecting the oceans proved to be so difficult?

    A   Many people do not accept that there is a serious problem.
    B   The legal situation is not recognised equally around the world.
    C   The activities of the fishing industry often obstruct conservation.

6 In the speaker's opinion, conservation projects that focus on individual species

    A   fail to take wider implications into account.
    B   cause confusion about the issues facing environmentalists.
    C   provide misleading information for publication.

Part 2

You will hear a talk about a Chinese animal called the giant panda.

For questions **7–15**, complete the sentences with a word or short phrase.

_____

The speaker expresses surprise that the giant panda has sometimes been called a

(7) ....

The speaker says that experts sometimes regard the giant panda as a

(8) ....

The giant panda has an elongated wrist bone, which it uses like a

(9) ....

In addition to bamboo, the giant panda may eat some small creatures, as well as different types of

(10) ....

The giant panda leaves scent markings at territory boundaries which can indicate its

(11) .... as well as some physical details.

The giant panda shows hostility by making a **(12)** .... sound.

The giant panda now just lives in a few **(13)** .... regions of China.

The speaker mentions the importance of establishing areas called

(14) .... between giant panda habitats.

It has been suggested that the conservation status of the giant panda should be changed to

(15) ....

Part 3

You will hear part of a programme in which Amanda and Peter, two founders of a fruit juice company called Topfruit, talk about their business.

For questions **16–20**, choose the answer (**A, B, C** or **D**) which fits best according to what you hear.

16 What opinion is expressed about the way Topfruit was set up?

   A   It is surprising that it worked out so smoothly.

   B   Working with friends certainly saved time and energy.

   C   Having a single founder would have made the launch simpler.

   D   Since the founders had such similar views it was hard to allocate roles.

17 What is the positive culture of the company mainly attributed to?

   A   guaranteed salary increases

   B   the nature of the product that is being sold

   C   strict adherence to staff monitoring procedures

   D   certain criteria in the recruitment process

18 How do both founders feel about running their company now?

   A   They are fed up with dealing with daily problems.

   B   They feel anxious about whether its success will continue.

   C   They enjoy the challenges they face in their work.

   D   They feel pleased that they have acquired a good grasp of business.

19 When describing past mistakes in staffing, Amanda reveals

   A   her belief that good qualifications are the key factor.

   B   her acceptance that it is vital to admit failures early on.

   C   her trust that improvements can be made to the process.

   D   her fear that senior appointments are impossible to get right.

20 What gives Topfruit an advantage over its larger competitors?

   A   The emphasis on ingredients which fit market trends.

   B   The product research based on scientific models.

   C   The clarity of the labelling.

   D   The extremely sophisticated advertising.

Part 4

You will hear five short extracts in which some sportspeople are talking about their sporting successes.

TASK ONE

For questions **21–25**, choose from the list **(A–H)** what each speaker regards as the key to winning in sport.

TASK TWO

For questions **26–30**, choose from the list **(A–H)** what each speaker sees their coach as.

While you listen, you must complete both tasks.

A stamina	**A** a risk taker
B a competitive training environment	**B** a role model
C team spirit	**C** a resource
D a natural ability	**D** a pioneer
E attention to detail	**E** a motivator
F anticipation	**F** a traditionalist
G taking advantage of luck	**G** a disciplinarian
H intimidation	**H** a facilitator

Speaker 1	21		Speaker 1	26
Speaker 2	22		Speaker 2	27
Speaker 3	23		Speaker 3	28
Speaker 4	24		Speaker 4	29
Speaker 5	25		Speaker 5	30

SPEAKING (16 minutes)

There are two examiners. One (the interlocutor) conducts the test, providing you with the necessary materials and explaining what you have to do. The other examiner (the assessor) will be introduced to you, but then takes no further part in the interaction.

Part 1 (2 minutes)

The interlocutor first asks you and your partner a few questions which focus on information about yourselves and personal opinions.

Part 2 (4 minutes)

In this part of the test you and your partner are asked to talk together. The interlocutor places a set of pictures on the table in front of you. There may be only one picture in the set or as many as seven pictures. This stimulus provides the basis for a discussion. The interlocutor first asks an introductory question which focuses on two of the pictures (or in the case of a single picture, on aspects of the picture). After about a minute, the interlocutor gives you both a decision-making task based on the same set of pictures.

The pictures for Part 2 are on pages C8–C9 of the colour section.

Part 3 (10 minutes)

You are each given the opportunity to talk for two minutes, to comment after your partner has spoken and to take part in a more general discussion.

The interlocutor gives you a card with a question written on it and asks you to talk about it for two minutes. After you have spoken, the interlocutor asks you both another question related to the topic on the card, addressing your partner first. This procedure is repeated, so that your partner receives a card and speaks for two minutes and a follow-up question is asked.

Finally, the interlocutor asks some further questions, which leads to a discussion on a general theme related to the subjects already covered in Part 3.

The cards for Part 3 are on pages C10–C11 of the colour section.

UNIVERSITY *of* CAMBRIDGE
ESOL Examinations

Do not write in this box

Candidate Name
If not already printed, write name
in CAPITALS and complete the
Candidate No. grid (in pencil).

Candidate Signature

Examination Title

Centre

Supervisor:
If the candidate is ABSENT or has WITHDRAWN shade here

SPECIMEN

Centre No.

Candidate No.

**Examination
Details**

0	0	0	0
1	1	1	1
2	2	2	2
3	3	3	3
4	4	4	4
5	5	5	5
6	6	6	6
7	7	7	7
8	8	8	8
9	9	9	9

Candidate Answer Sheet 1

Instructions

Use a PENCIL (B or HB). Rub out any answer you wish to change using an eraser.

Part 1: Mark ONE letter for each question.

For example, if you think **B** is the right
answer to the question, mark your
answer sheet like this:

0 A B C D

Parts 2, 3 and **4:** Write your answer clearly
in CAPITAL LETTERS.

For Parts 2 and 3 write one letter
in each box. For example:

0 E X A M P L E

Part 1

1	A	B	C	D
2	A	B	C	D
3	A	B	C	D
4	A	B	C	D
5	A	B	C	D
6	A	B	C	D
7	A	B	C	D
8	A	B	C	D

Part 2

Do not write
below here

9		9 1 0 u
10		10 1 0 u
11		11 1 0 u
12		12 1 0 u
13		13 1 0 u
14		14 1 0 u
15		15 1 0 u
16		16 1 0 u

Continues over ➡

CPE R1

DP690/190

© UCLES 2012 Photocopiable

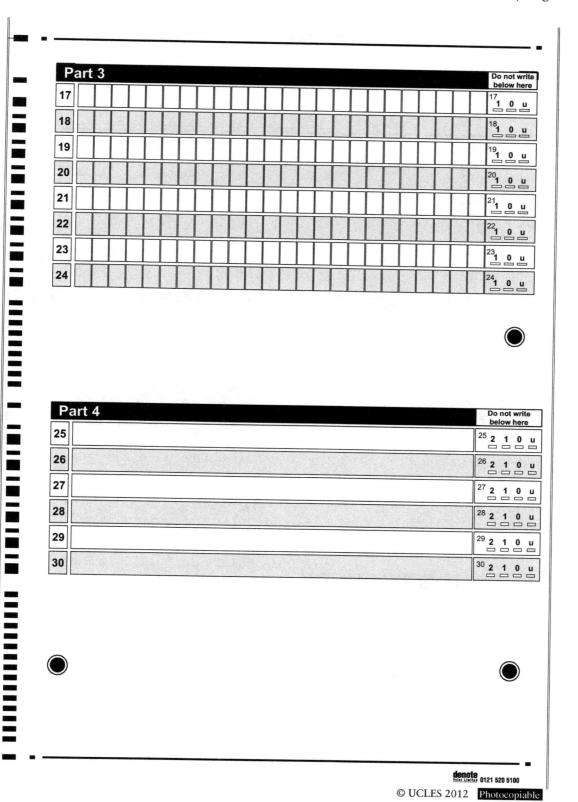

denote Print Limited 0121 520 5100

© UCLES 2012 Photocopiable

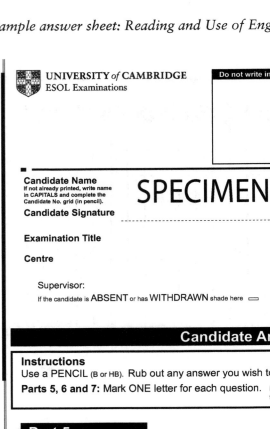

UNIVERSITY *of* CAMBRIDGE
ESOL Examinations

Do not write in this box

SPECIMEN

Candidate Name
If not already printed, write name
in CAPITALS and complete the
Candidate No. grid (in pencil).

Candidate Signature

Examination Title

Centre

Supervisor:
If the candidate is ABSENT or has WITHDRAWN shade here ▭

Centre No.

Candidate No.

Examination
Details

Candidate Answer Sheet 2

Instructions
Use a PENCIL (B or HB). Rub out any answer you wish to change using an eraser.

Parts 5, 6 and 7: Mark ONE letter for each question. For example, if you think **B** is the right answer to the question, mark your answer sheet like this:

Part 5

31	A	B	C	D
32	A	B	C	D
33	A	B	C	D
34	A	B	C	D
35	A	B	C	D
36	A	B	C	D

Part 6

37	A	B	C	D	E	F	G	H
38	A	B	C	D	E	F	G	H
39	A	B	C	D	E	F	G	H
40	A	B	C	D	E	F	G	H
41	A	B	C	D	E	F	G	H
42	A	B	C	D	E	F	G	H
43	A	B	C	D	E	F	G	H

Part 7

44	A	B	C	D	E	F
45	A	B	C	D	E	F
46	A	B	C	D	E	F
47	A	B	C	D	E	F
48	A	B	C	D	E	F
49	A	B	C	D	E	F
50	A	B	C	D	E	F
51	A	B	C	D	E	F
52	A	B	C	D	E	F
53	A	B	C	D	E	F

CPE R2

denote Print Limited 0121 520 5100

DP691/191

© UCLES 2012 Photocopiable

UNIVERSITY *of* **CAMBRIDGE**
ESOL Examinations

Do not write in this box

Candidate Name
If not already printed, write name in CAPITALS and complete the Candidate No. grid (in pencil).

Candidate Signature

Examination Title

Centre

Supervisor:
If the candidate is ABSENT or has WITHDRAWN shade here ▭

Test version: A B C D E F J K L M N   Special arrangements: S H

SPECIMEN

Centre No.

Candidate No.

Examination Details

0	0	0	0
1	1	1	1
2	2	2	2
3	3	3	3
4	4	4	4
5	5	5	5
6	6	6	6
7	7	7	7
8	8	8	8
9	9	9	9

Candidate Answer Sheet

Instructions

Use a PENCIL (B or HB).
Rub out any answer you wish to change using an eraser.

Parts 1, 3 and **4:**
Mark ONE letter for each question.

For example, if you think **B** is the right answer to the question, mark your answer sheet like this:

| 0 | A | B | C |

Part 2:
Write your answer clearly in CAPITAL LETTERS.

Write one letter or number in each box.
If the answer has more than one word, leave one box empty between words.

For example:

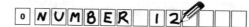

| 0 | N | U | M | B | E | R | | 1 | 2 | | | |

Turn this sheet over to start.

DP692/192

© UCLES 2012 Photocopiable

Part 1

1	A	B	C
2	A	B	C
3	A	B	C
4	A	B	C
5	A	B	C
6	A	B	C

Part 2 (Remember to write in CAPITAL LETTERS or numbers)

Do not write below here

7	7 1 0 u
8	8 1 0 u
9	9 1 0 u
10	10 1 0 u
11	11 1 0 u
12	12 1 0 u
13	13 1 0 u
14	14 1 0 u
15	15 1 0 u

Part 3

16	A	B	C	D
17	A	B	C	D
18	A	B	C	D
19	A	B	C	D
20	A	B	C	D

Part 4

21	A	B	C	D	E	F	G	H
22	A	B	C	D	E	F	G	H
23	A	B	C	D	E	F	G	H
24	A	B	C	D	E	F	G	H
25	A	B	C	D	E	F	G	H
26	A	B	C	D	E	F	G	H
27	A	B	C	D	E	F	G	H
28	A	B	C	D	E	F	G	H
29	A	B	C	D	E	F	G	H
30	A	B	C	D	E	F	G	H

denote Print Limited 0121 520 5100

© UCLES 2012 Photocopiable

Visual materials for the Speaking test

1A

1B

1C

1D

Magazine survey – Annoyances

2A

2B

2C

2D

2E

2F

3A

The 2008 Beijing Olympic Games, China - 18 Aug 2008 Silver medallist Jacqueline Lawrence of Australia, gold medallist Elena Kaliska of Slovakia and bronze medallist Violetta Oblinger Peters of Austria celebrate on the podium after the Women's Kayak (K1) Finals event

3B

3C

3D

3E

4A

4B

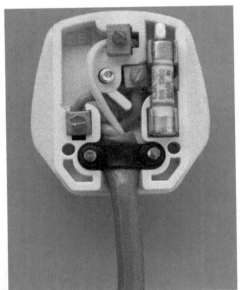

4C

4D

4E

TEST 1

Prompt card 1a

To what extent do professional sportsmen and women need support?

- from trainers
- from the public
- from governments

TEST 2

Prompt card 2a

What creates a positive learning environment?

- people
- resources
- mood

TEST 3

Prompt card 3a

Why is it important to celebrate special dates?

- for an individual
- for a family
- for a country

TEST 4

Prompt card 4a

How much do we know about the food we eat?

- origins
- production
- labelling

TEST 1

Prompt card 1b

How important is it for effort to be recognised?

- for children
- at work
- in the arts

TEST 2

Prompt card 2b

Why do people explore the world around them?

- holidays
- business
- science

TEST 3

Prompt card 3b

How do our priorities change at different stages of life?

- relationships
- ambition
- possessions

TEST 4

Prompt card 4b

What responsibilities do governments have with regard to people's health?

- medicine
- at work
- leisure facilities